THE WIZARD OF OZ:
THE SCREENPLAY

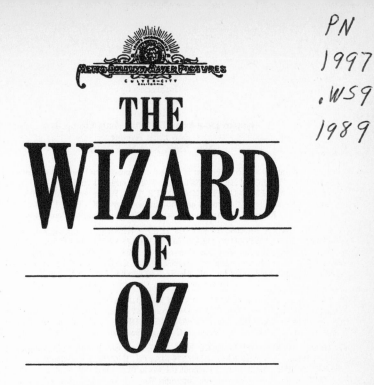

THE
WIZARD
OF
OZ

THE SCREENPLAY

*Published by arrangement with
Turner Entertainment Co.*

By

Noel Langley, Florence Ryerson
& Edgar Allan Woolf

From the Book by
L. FRANK BAUM

Edited with an Introduction by
MICHAEL PATRICK HEARN

A Delta Book
Published by
Dell Publishing
a division of
Bantam Doubleday Dell Publishing Group, Inc.
666 Fifth Avenue
New York, New York 10103

Designed by Richard Oriolo

Library of Congress Cataloging in Publication Data
Langley, Noel, 1911–
    The wizard of Oz: the screenplay / by Noel Langley, Florence
Ryerson, and Edgar Allan Woolf; from the book by Frank Baum;
edited with an introduction by Michael Patrick Hearn.
    p.   cm.
    ISBN 0-385-29760-2
    1. Wizard of Oz (Motion picture)   I. Ryerson, Florence.
II. Woolf, Edgar Allan.   III. Hearn, Michael Patrick.   IV. Baum,
L. Frank (Lyman Frank). Wizard of Oz.   V. Title.
PN1997.W59   1989
791.43'72—dc19   89-1306
                                                                CIP

Printed in the United States of America
Published simultaneously in Canada

August 1989

10 9 8 7 6 5 4 3 2 1
BG

For
my favorite Munchkins—
Emily,
Elysia,
Kayleigh,
and
Caroline.

M.P.H.

ACKNOWLEDGMENTS

The principal source for information on the 1939 movie is Aljean Harmetz's *The Making of the Wizard of Oz* (1977; 1989). Mervyn LeRoy's memoirs, *Mervyn LeRoy: Take One* (1974); Edward Jablonski's *Harold Arlen: Happy with the Blues* (1961); and Hugh Fordin's survey of Arthur Freed's career, *The World of Entertainment* (1975), were also helpful. I am also indebted to John Fricke, who so graciously took time from his own study *The Wizard of Oz: The Official Fiftieth Anniversary Pictorial History* (1989), coauthored with Jay Scarfone and William Stillman, to provide me with invaluable information and rare material. Other assistance was generously given by Robert A. Baum, Jr., David Brooks, Bruce and Gail Crockett, Karl Michael Emyrs, Michael Gessel, Ernest Harburg, Aljean Harmetz, Edward Jablonski, Michael Kerker, Marc Lewis, Tod Machin, Nick Markovich, Dorothy Maryott, Dan Patterson, Bronson Pinchot, Dan and Lynne Smith, Richard Warren, and Barbara Zitwer. The public collections consulted for this book were the Margaret Herrick Library at the Academy of Motion Picture Arts and Sciences; the University of Southern California Archives of the Performing Arts, the University of Southern California at Los Angeles; the Billy Rose Collection, the New York Public Library at Lincoln Center; the Film Study Center, the Museum of Modern Art; E. Y. Harburg Papers, the Yale Collection of the Literature of the American Musical Theater, Yale University Library; Turner Entertainment Co.; and the Library of Congress. I am also grateful to Robert Miller and Mitchell Rose, particularly for their patience. And finally I wish to thank Carole Orgel and Lois Sloane of Turner Entertainment Co. for arranging for the publication of the screenplay of *The Wizard of Oz* on the fiftieth anniversary of its release.

M.P.H.

THE WIZARD OF OZ:
THE SCREENPLAY

INTRODUCTION

It was not the first. Only a few months after the publication of *The Wonderful Wizard of Oz* in Chicago in 1900, L. Frank Baum was hard at work dramatizing his best-selling children's story. A young composer named Paul Tietjens, whom Baum had met through the book's illustrator, William Wallace Denslow, suggested that the fairy tale would make a fine musical play, and the two quickly prepared a libretto and a number of songs to show possible producers. Denslow, who was co-owner of the book's copyright and thus had an interest in its staging, arranged with the owner of Chicago's Grand Opera House for a summer showing. Unfortunately the man chosen to direct the production threw out most of Tietjens' score and drew up an entirely new scenario, from which Baum had to write a new libretto. He also hired other songwriters and script doctors to help shape it for the stage.

When *The Wizard of Oz* opened on June 16, 1902, it bore little resemblance to Baum's fairy tale. Dorothy was now a young woman falling in and out of love and accompanied on her travels through Oz by her pet cow, Imogene. A secondary plot entailed a battle over the throne of Oz between the Wizard and a trolley-car conductor from Topeka. There was no Wicked Witch of the West, and the Wizard himself, by the time the play reached Broadway in January 1903, became a wisecracking Irishman. Nevertheless *The Wizard of Oz* proved to be one of the most successful plays of its day, due to its magnificent staging and memorable performances rather than to its weak score and sometimes incomprehensible libretto. This musical extravaganza entered American theatrical history for its lavish transformation scenes—the Kansas Cyclone, the Wizard's Palace, and (most beautiful of all) the Deadly Poppy Field, in which the pretty chorus girls, dressed as the poisonous flowers, were destroyed by the Good Witch's snowstorm each night on stage. The true hits of the show, however, were the former vaudevillians Fred A. Stone and David C. Montgomery as the Scarecrow and the Tin Man.

The Wizard of Oz toured the country for eight years and inspired countless imitations as well as a long series of Oz books. The first of these, *The Marvelous Land of Oz* (1904), appropriately dedicated to Montgomery and Stone, Baum turned into another musical extravaganza called *The Woggle Bug* in 1905, but it was a financial failure. Baum tried once more to recapture the success of *The Wizard of Oz* by adapting elements from several of his Oz stories as *The Tik-Tok Man of Oz* in Los Angeles in 1913. This musical had a reasonable run on the West Coast and throughout the Midwest.

Baum also recognized the vast potential of the early motion picture. On a trip to Paris in 1906 he was introduced to a new but primitive form of color photography, and upon his return to Chicago he devised a novel way of exploiting the process to promote his children's books. He toured the country in 1908 and 1909 in his *Fairylogue and Radio-Plays,** a lecture tour combining hand-colored slides and trick films of various scenes from his fairy tales. Baum financed the venture himself and rented William N. Selig's motion picture studio in Chicago to shoot the movie portion of the program, which employed early methods of trick photography. Unfortunately the enormous costs of production far exceeded Baum's box office receipts, and the failure of the *Fairylogue and Radio-Plays* eventually forced Baum to file for bankruptcy. In part to pay off his debts, he turned over the film rights of several of his children's stories to Selig, who issued a series of Oz pictures in 1910, including a one-reeler of *The Wonderful Wizard of Oz.*

By then, Baum and his wife had settled in the then quiet suburb of Hollywood, where he literally saw the infant motion picture industry grow up around him. In 1914 he founded the Oz Film Manufacturing Company to produce silent movies of his various books. (One of these, *His Majesty, the Scarecrow of Oz,* borrowed some elements from the first Oz book, so when the picture was released in early 1915, it was renamed *The New Wizard of Oz.*) But Baum quickly

* The term *Radio-play* refers to Michel Radio, the inventor of the early color film process, and not to wireless transmission.

learned that it was far easier to make movies than to get them distributed, and his production company closed within a year of its founding, with only a half dozen completed films, some of which were never released.

But L. Frank Baum was primarily a children's book writer, not a playwright, not a filmmaker. By the time of his death in 1919, he had completed fourteen Oz books, which proved to be among the biggest juvenile best-sellers of the time. The series was so successful that the publishers could not let it end with their author's death, so they contracted with his widow, Maud Gage Baum, to have the stories continued by another writer, Ruth Plumly Thompson. Disgruntled that *he* had not been asked to carry on his father's work, Baum's oldest son, Frank Joslyn Baum, secured from his mother permission to sell certain rights to the books for the estate. But first he had to clear up all the conflicting claims to the Oz series that had resulted from his father's bankruptcy and defunct film company. Once all the copyrights to the books, plays, and motion pictures were finally returned to the family, Frank J. Baum sold the silent film rights of *The Wizard of Oz* to a minor production company, Chadwick Pictures Corporation. In 1925, they released a dismal slapstick comedy under that name, starring Larry Semon as the Scarecrow and Oliver Hardy (before he met Stan Laurel) as the Tin Man. The scenario, cocredited to "L. Frank Baum, Jr.," abandoned Baum's fairy tale to tell a new story of how Dorothy, now a flapper from Kansas, is restored to the throne of Oz. The Scarecrow, Tin Man, and Cowardly Lion appeared only briefly and as disguises for three Kansas farm hands; and the whole film was framed as a largely inappropriate bedtime story for a little girl.

The Chadwick picture was not successful and was quickly forgotten. In 1928 Mrs. Baum allowed Samuel French to publish a children's theater play of *The Wizard of Oz* by Elizabeth Fuller Goodrich, to be performed by the Junior League and other amateur groups. She also successfully negotiated through the publishers for a *Wizard of Oz* radio program, sponsored by Jell-O gelatin and aired by the National Broadcasting Company three times a week between September 25, 1933, and March 23, 1934.

In the meantime, Frank J. Baum was aggressively offering the film rights around Hollywood. With the coming of sound in 1927, the motion picture industry was eagerly buying up old musical comedy properties, and many executives remembered the Montgomery and Stone play of *The Wizard of Oz* or had grown up on the books. A number of studios considered, and some even purchased options on, the Oz stories, but surprisingly little was done with them for years. United Productions did produce a short called *The Scarecrow of Oz* (1931) featuring the Ethel Meglin Kiddies, a well-known Hollywood children's theatrical company that at one time included both Shirley Temple and Judy Garland; and in 1933, the talented animator Ted Eshbaugh, best remembered for *The Sunshine Makers* (1935) for the Van Beuren Studio, completed an amusing one-reel cartoon of *The Wizard of Oz*, cowritten by "Col. Frank Baum," but it was never distributed because of a dispute with Technicolor, which had filmed it. Ruth Plumly Thompson tried to interest Walt Disney in making animated cartoons based on the Oz books, but Mrs. Baum eventually turned him down, calling him "dishonest."* Instead she sold the animation rights to a puppeteer named Kenneth L. McLellan, who never found the financial backing for his proposed shorts.

Frank J. Baum was more successful with Samuel Goldwyn. He envisioned *The Wizard of Oz* as a Technicolor musical with Eddie Cantor as the Scarecrow. On January 26, 1934, Goldwyn bought the film rights to *The Wizard of Oz* from Baum for $40,000. Unfortunately, by that time Cantor's Hollywood career was waning, and Goldwyn did nothing with the property for several years.

Metro-Goldwyn-Mayer considered making a movie of *The Wizard of Oz* as early as 1924, when Frank J. Baum was peddling the silent film rights. But growing impatient with the studio's legal department, Baum withdrew his offer and sold the rights to Chadwick Pictures instead. Then, in 1933, following the Eshbaugh debacle and while Baum was negotiating with Goldwyn for a musical comedy feature, MGM wanted to option the Oz books for a series of animated cartoons. Again Baum and the producers could not agree on terms. In

---

* It was not until after Mrs. Baum's death, in 1954, that Walt Disney did buy the film rights to all of her husband's Oz books except the first. The studio considered making a musical called *The Rainbow Road to Oz*, to feature the Mouseketeers; a few numbers for the proposed movie were performed on "The Fourth Anniversary Show" on *Disneyland*, on September 11, 1957. (Instead they produced in 1961 a poor adaptation of Victor Herbert's *Babes in Toyland*, with Annette Funicello and Ray Bolger.) In 1985, Walt Disney Pictures finally released *Return to Oz*, a humorless and sometimes disturbing vision of the Land of Oz, directed by Walter Murch.

1937, when MGM was founding its own cartoon studio under Fred Quimby, the company once more looked into the possibility of buying rights to all of the Oz stories but the first (now Goldwyn's property) for animated shorts. However, Howard Dietz, the lyricist and then head of publicity at Loew's, queried librarians and booksellers on the proposed series and was informed that Oz cartoons would *not* appeal to adults. Instead MGM bought the rights to King Features' popular comic strip "The Captain and the Kids."

In 1937 the studio was in transition. Since its formation in 1924, Metro-Goldwyn-Mayer had risen to become the leading motion picture company in Hollywood. Its reputation for making the best movies in America was generally attributed, rightly or wrongly, to its young producer, Irving G. Thalberg. But Thalberg died in 1936, and Louis B. Mayer hired Mervyn LeRoy to replace him. At Warner Bros., LeRoy had directed several of the most influential films of the early sound era, including *Little Caesar* (1930) and *I Am a Fugitive from a Chain Gang* (1932), but he had limited experience as a movie producer. Also Arthur Freed, who had written with composer Nacio Herb Brown the scores for such successful MGM musicals as *The Broadway Melody* (1929), and *Broadway Melody of 1936* (1935), their most famous song being "Singin' in the Rain," now wanted to produce. When Mayer asked LeRoy and Freed which book each man would like to film, both replied, *"The Wizard of Oz."*

But Goldwyn still owned the rights, and MGM was only one of several studios now interested in the property. Because Walt Disney's *Snow White and the Seven Dwarfs* had proven to be one of the most successful pictures of 1937, the industry began aggressively seeking other suitable fantasy subjects to film. Twentieth Century-Fox was especially interested in *The Wizard of Oz* for its biggest box office star, Shirley Temple. But MGM outbid the others, and although Goldwyn had left Metro in 1922, the transferral of rights was relatively easy. On June 3, 1938, Goldwyn officially sold *The Wizard of Oz* to Loew's, Incorporated, MGM's parent company, for $75,000, which (as LeRoy later stated) "must go down alongside the Louisiana Purchase as one of the biggest bargains of all times."

Before MGM would sign anything, the legal department spent months making exhaustive inquiries into any possible claimant from any previous stage or screen adaption of Baum's book, checking everyone from Goldwyn to the executrix of W. W. Denslow's estate. In effect, what the studio finally purchased was permission to use, in addition to the original children's story, material from any previous commercial dramatization of the book. The lawyers were also concerned over the status of the remaining Oz titles: they feared unwanted competition should the Baum family permit someone else to make motion pictures of other books, such as *The Marvelous Land of Oz* (1904), *Dorothy and the Wizard in Oz* (1908), and *The Scarecrow of Oz* (1915), and utilize characters who also appeared in *The Wizard of Oz*. MGM, therefore, offered Maud Baum $50,000 for the film rights to the remaining series, but fully aware of what the studio had paid for *The Wizard of Oz*, she declined. She had little hope for the proposed movie. She wrote Ruth Plumly Thompson in March, "I will never believe *The Wizard* will be produced until I see it on the screen—I'm from Missouri." When LeRoy asked Mrs. Baum what she expected of the picture, she recalled the previous films of her husband's work and told him, "Oh, I suppose there'll be a Wizard in it, and a Scarecrow and a Tin Woodman, and maybe a Lion and a character named Dorothy. But that's all I expect, young man. You see, I've lived in Hollywood since 1910."

While both wanted to make *The Wizard of Oz*, Mayer finally settled on LeRoy over Freed. It was just too expensive a project to entrust to a novice. LeRoy, however, knew relatively little about musical comedy—certainly less than Freed. He had directed a few at Warner Bros., the most famous being *Gold Diggers of 1933*, but the lavish musical numbers in that picture ("We're in the Money," "Remember My Forgotten Man") had been staged by Busby Berkeley. Although he did not receive screen credit for his considerable contribution to the making of *The Wizard of Oz*, Freed did serve his apprenticeship as a producer while working under LeRoy on that film. For LeRoy, *The Wizard of Oz* proved to be "one gigantic headache."

While concentrating on other numerous preproduction details, LeRoy turned the book over to his assistant, William Cannon, in early January, to get his thoughts on how best to dramatize the story. Cannon wisely advised that the picture not be a period piece but reflect a contemporary view of fairyland. He also expressed a niggling Hollywood aversion to fantasy. Recent attempts at fairy tales with live actors had been disappointing: Paramount's all-star *Alice in*

Wonderland (1933) had been a box office disaster, despite W. C. Fields as Humpty Dumpty, Gary Cooper as the White Knight, and Cary Grant as the Mock Turtle; likewise Warner Bros.' *A Midsummer Night's Dream* (1935), magnificently staged by Max Reinhardt, had done no better, even with James Cagney as Bottom, Joe E. Brown as Flute, Dick Powell as Lysander, and Mickey Rooney as Puck. It was then generally conceded that the only one in Hollywood who could successfully film fairy tales was Walt Disney.

Cannon insisted that magic be used only sparingly throughout the movie. He also believed that the public would never accept a live Scarecrow and a live Tin Man, arguing that they must merely be (as in the 1925 Chadwick picture) people disguised as a Scarecrow and a Tin Man. Although LeRoy and Freed rejected this last suggestion, a certain literal-mindedness lingered throughout the production.

In the meantime LeRoy, who had loved the story as a boy, reread the book and marked passages in his copy to be dramatized. The development of the script, however, eventually became largely Freed's responsibility. Work on the screenplay began in earnest months before MGM and Goldwyn finally signed their contract. The first of the dozen screenwriters consulted on *The Wizard of Oz* was Irving Brecher, who had previously collaborated with LeRoy at Warner Bros., notably on *Fools for Scandal* (1938) with Carole Lombard, but Brecher was immediately taken off *The Wizard of Oz* to begin *At the Circus* (1939), which LeRoy was producing for the Marx Brothers.

The next one to work on *The Wizard of Oz* was Herman J. Mankiewicz. Assigned on February 28 and removed on March 23, Mankiewicz was an odd choice to adapt a children's story. This former member of the Algonquin Round Table in New York City was considered one of the wittiest men in Hollywood; he was a producer as well as a screenwriter and known for his highly sophisticated comedies, the best being *Dinner at Eight* (1933) for MGM. He did turn in an incomplete script for *The Wizard of Oz* (not going far past the introduction of the Cowardly Lion, here on all fours) that was principally a patchwork of dialogue and description taken from Baum's book. One of his major objections to the original story was the depiction of Dorothy's foster parents. "It is enough that Aunt Em, like Uncle Henry, is worn by toil," Mankiewicz noted, "but it can serve no purpose, and can do actual harm that they be professional joy-killers." Unfortunately the opening scene he wrote for them is uncharacteristically insipid. More successful is his handling of Dorothy's first encounters with the Scarecrow and the Tin Man, which do capture the "naive simplicity" Mankiewicz admired in Baum's writing.

Of course, in adapting the familiar children's story to musical comedy conventions, Mankiewicz (like Baum himself in 1902) had to include gratuitous characters and incidents not always in harmony with the original fairy tale. The screenwriter was also expected to tailor his script to the particular talents of certain players already under contract to MGM. From the start Freed saw *The Wizard of Oz* as the perfect vehicle to further the screen career of his fifteen-year-old protégée Judy Garland, with whom he had already worked on *Thoroughbreds Don't Cry* (1937) and *Broadway Melody of 1938* (1937). He also wanted to create parts for two other young performers, Betty Jaynes and Kenny Baker. Garland, therefore, was to be Dorothy, "an orphan from Kansas who sings jazz," and Jaynes to be Princess Betty of Oz, "who sings opera" and is in love with Grand Duke Alan, to be portrayed by Baker. Now Dorothy was off to see the Wizard not only to get home but also to rescue this royal Munchkin couple imprisoned by the Wicked Witch of the West.

Mankiewicz also added some satirical asides to Baum's narrative. His Wicked Witch of the West runs an office behind "an American businessman's desk" and a frosted glass door that reads:

WICKED WITCH OF THE WEST
Cruelties, Tortures
and all kinds of
Devilments
Decent People Keep Out!
This Means You!

Consequently, in Mankiewicz's script, she is as comic as she is malevolent; her chief threat is sneezing people to death. Dorothy also cracks topical jokes: The only wizards she knows back in Kansas are "oil wizards and wheat wizards"; she explains to Toto a major difference between Oz and Kansas: "Here, if you've got no brains, they stuff you and make you a scarecrow—but back home, Uncle Henry used to say that if you had no brains, you could always go to work for the government." Also there is a long, tiresome scene in Kansas in which Dorothy betters a rich little girl with a chauffeur and a Pekingese named Adolphus Ajax Rittenstaufen the Third, who stop by the farm on the way to Santa Barbara. All in all, Mankiewicz's script was a halfhearted effort and rejected by the studio. The writer's erratic behavior due to too much drinking and compulsive gambling offended Mayer, and his contract was not renewed later that year. But Mankiewicz did return to Hollywood the following year with an original screenplay for RKO—*Citizen Kane* (1941).

Despite its flaws, Mankiewicz's adaptation of *The Wizard of Oz* did contain elements eventually woven into the final film: a lengthy Kansas prologue; the Munchkins to be played by midgets; the Wicked Witch of the West as a threat from the moment of Dorothy's arrival in Oz. Also several of the musical numbers were already suggested in this early script: Dorothy's Kansas song; the celebration of the Munchkins; special song-and-dance routines for the Scarecrow and the Tin Man. But the most important section of Mankiewicz's script to remain in the produced movie was the transition from Kansas to fairyland by contrasting the grayness of the farm with the colorful atmosphere of Oz, just as Baum had described it in his book. "As we discussed," Mankiewicz noted, "this part of the picture—until the door is flung open after Dorothy has arrived in the land of the Munchkins—will be shot in black and white." Clearly from the start the producers had decided to film the Kansas sequences in monochrome and those in Oz in Technicolor. Mankiewicz also warned the studio about Dorothy and Toto in the prologue: "Only one thing is vital—neither of them dares be gray."*

It was common practice in Hollywood at the time to assign several screenwriters to the same project, often working simultaneously but independently of one another. Then the producers had to shape the final screenplay from their various versions. Even before Mankiewicz

* At one point during the production the special-effects department considered keeping Dorothy in black and white in Munchkinland until the Good Witch changes her to color. *The Wizard of Oz* was not the only MGM movie to combine black-and-white and color footage; for example, *The Broadway Melody* (1929) included a primitive two-color sequence for "The Wedding of the Painted Doll," and George Cukor filmed a fashion show in Technicolor in *The Women* and LeRoy inserted a lavish production number in color in *Ice Follies of 1939,* both released in 1939.

had been taken off *The Wizard of Oz,* two other writers were given the story to dramatize. Ogden Nash, the noted author of light verse who had also worked on *The Firefly* (1937) for MGM, was with the production from March 7 through April 16, but made no important contribution to the script. He was joined on March 11 by Noel Langley, a playwright and author of a charming children's story, *The Tale of the Land of Green Ginger* (1937) by "Arthur Barber," about the Arabian Nights' adventures of Aladdin's son. Langley was also valued by the studio for having prepared a usable screenplay for the musical *Maytime* (1937) in just three and a half days. In the meantime still another writer, Herbert Fields (who had also worked on *Fools for Scandal*), was assigned between April 19 and 22, but produced nothing of consequence.

The Wizard of Oz was not easy. Langley's first treatment took extraordinary liberties with the children's book. Born in South Africa, the young screenwriter had not been brought up on the Oz series, but he did bring a remarkable recollection of other juvenile literature and silent motion pictures to his interpretation of Baum's American fairy tale. Langley's most alarming violation of Baum's text was the explaining of Dorothy's trip to Oz as no more than a dream. Of course this device was as old as Lewis Carroll's *Alice's Adventures in Wonderland,* first published in England in 1865, but Baum, fully aware of his predecessor's efforts, did not want the source for his fantasy to be as prosaic as Carroll's. Langley, however, agreed with Cannon that no modern audience would accept Dorothy's companions unless they were first introduced as human beings. He therefore justified the grotesque characters in Oz as distortions of people back in Kansas. Langley said that he got the idea from an old Mary Pickford picture, *The Poor Little Rich Girl* (1917), in which the child's servants reappear in a nightmare in various bizarre forms, but Langley may also have had in mind the 1925 Chadwick movie of *The Wizard in Oz,* in which the Kansas farm hands later dress up as the Scarecrow, the Tin Man, and the Cowardly Lion. By 1939 this plot twist was almost a cinematic cliché; for example, there was also a dream sequence in the Shirley Temple movie *The Little Princess* in which the people she knows in London become fairy tale characters.

Langley invented an elaborate scheme for his prologue in typical musical comedy fashion that bore as little relation to the children's story as Baum's 1902 play did. Dorothy was now romantically linked to the farm hand Hickory, who becomes the Scarecrow; the Tin Man is another farm hand named Hunk* in love with Lizzie Smithers, who works in a soda parlor in Kansas and as the Wizard's assistant in Oz; the Wicked Witch is Miss Gulch, Dorothy's schoolteacher; and, oddest of all, Uncle Henry becomes the Witch's son, Bulbo, taken from William Makepeace Thackeray's burlesque fairy tale *The Rose and the Ring* (1855). Betty Jaynes and Kenny Baker were not forgotten in Langley's summary: They are now Sylvia, the Witch's beautiful prisoner, and her lover Florizel, whom the Witch has transformed into the Cowardly Lion. LeRoy wanted a simpler prologue: Dorothy while reading *The Wizard of Oz* in bed, is struck on the head by a falling book that sends her dreaming. But Fred preferred Langley's suggestion.

Once Dorothy gets to Oz, Langley's treatment generally follows Baum's plot as far as the Emerald City. (Langley did introduce the Good Witch in a great bubble, the mode of transport of the underwater witch in an obscure Annette Kellerman picture of 1918, *Queen of the Sea,* a silent version of Hans Christian Andersen's "The Little Mermaid.") Unfortunately Langley had the Wizard immediately exposed as a humbug on Dorothy's first meeting, and from that point Langley largely forgot Baum's story: Dorothy and her friends, now accompanied by the Wizard and Lizzie Smithers, go disguised as a traveling circus to stir up a revolution against the Witch; and Florizel battles a dragon and conquers the Witch in an aerial dog fight by hacking away at her broom.

While much of Langley's treatment was unusable, Freed nevertheless preferred his to any of the others and authorized him to write a screenplay. He still needed considerable guidance. The plot he devised was unnecessarily complicated, with too many conflicting motivations for the characters—Dorothy wants to get home and is in love with Hickory, the Wicked Witch covets Dorothy's shoes and plans to conquer the Emerald City. Freed thought that the Witch should be a greater antagonist to Dorothy, that the Witch's conflict with the

* The names of the farm hands were switched in the script when Ray Bolger and Buddy Ebsen, originally cast as the Tin Man and the Scarecrow, exchanged roles; Ebsen was replaced by Jack Haley two weeks into shooting after he developed an allergy to the metallic makeup.

Wizard should be secondary to hers with Dorothy. "We must remember at all times," Freed reminded Langley, "that Dorothy is only motivated by one object in Oz; that is, how to get back home to her Aunt Em, and every situation should be related to this main drive."

But the chief weakness so far, according to Freed, was the lack of "a solid and dramatic drive of Dorothy's adventures and purposes that will keep the audience rooting for her" throughout her trip to Oz. Freed was a sentimental man and demanded that Dorothy have a deep-rooted psychological need back home that would justify her actions in Oz. "In Kansas," he explained, "it is our problem to set up the story of Dorothy, who finds herself with a heart full of love eager to give it, but through circumstances and personalities, can apparently find none in return. In this dilemma of childish frustration, she is hit on the head in a real cyclone and through her unconscious self, she finds escape in her dream of Oz. There she is motivated by her generosity to help everyone first before her little orphan heart cries out for what she wants most of all (the love of Aunt Em)—'which represents to her the love of a mother she never knew.' " Freed thus instructed Langley that, "besides our laughs and novelty," the movie had to contain "a real assault on our hearts." Consequently Dorothy in the film became far more weepy than Baum's practical, determined little girl from Kansas.

Between April 5 and June 4, 1938, Langley wrote countless drafts. A major problem was to convincingly tie the prologue and epilogue to events and characters in Oz. He padded the dialogue with details foreshadowing Dorothy's dream: Hickory Twicker, called "dumb" by Uncle Henry, applies to agricultural college; Lizzie Smithers, now Aunt Em's kitchen help, accuses Hunk Andrews of being heartless when he flirts with another girl in the soda parlor; Hickory chews on a poppy stem and is warned that opium comes from poppies. Langley finally realized that it would be out of character to have Uncle Henry reappear as the Witch's son, so *Miss* Gulch became *Mrs.* Gulch, with an obnoxious son named Walter, who is now Bulbo in Oz. Freed did not care for Sylvia and Florizel and reminded Langley, "Their story should in some way affect Dorothy's life and the fulfillment of her desires in order to give it any dramatic interest." Therefore Langley introduced them earlier as Mrs. Gulch's niece and the girl's boyfriend, Kenny Armbruster (renamed Kenelin in Oz), to whose romance her nasty aunt is violently opposed. And finally the Wizard of Oz pops up at the end as Dr. Pink (later renamed Dr. Miffle), who tends to Dorothy's bump on the head.

Langley also reshifted episodes from Baum's book. The Fighting Trees became the ill-tempered apple trees whom Dorothy and the Scarecrow battle just prior to their discovery of the Tin Man. Langley also moved the Deadly Poppy Field a scene earlier, *before* the Cowardly Lion appears. (He also threw out the field mice, who in the book save Dorothy and her friends from the poisonous flowers, and restored the Good Witch's snowstorm from the 1902 musical, the only original stage business of that play to reappear in the 1939 film.) Langley also considered a quick glimpse of the Dainty China Country on the way to the Wicked Witch's castle, but the scene was soon dropped, being not only gratuitous but too difficult to film.

The greatest troubles with Langley's script arose the further it departed from Baum's story. The introduction of many parallel characters in Kansas unnecessarily complicated the adventures in Oz, particularly the search for the Wicked Witch of the West. The Wizard still confesses his fraud on the first visit to the Emerald City but to Dorothy alone, and he and she (and Lizzie Smithers) try to escape after he gives each of her three companions what he wishes. (It is now Dorothy who discloses that "they've had all the things they want all the time, they just need to *believe* they've got them!") Unfortunately, when the balloon goes off without the Wizard, the Winged Monkeys swoop down and capture Dorothy, Toto, and Lizzie for the Wicked Witch. The three friends, along with the Wizard, go to save them; the Cowardly Lion, by disposing of the Witch's gorilla, turns back into Prince Kenelin. And all ends happily back in Kansas— Mrs. Gulch's schoolhouse has been destroyed by the cyclone, Walter and his mother land in a water trough, Sylvia and Kenny in each other's arms, and Dorothy waves lovingly to Hickory from the train platform as he departs for agricultural college.

This first script was unfilmable, but the producers considered it salvageable and directed Langley through many rewrites. They brought in another script doctor, Samuel Hoffenstein, who had worked on such musicals as *Love Me Tonight* (1932) and *The Great Waltz* (1938), but he added nothing substantial to *The Wizard of Oz* during his brief tenure, between May 31 and June 3. Many of their problems could easily have been solved had they just gone back to Baum's book, but they had their own ideas, not all of them sound. For example, Freed could not see how the Winged Monkeys could be filmed and suggested instead that Dorothy encounter some physical upheaval in the Wicked Witch's country similar to the earthquake in *San Francisco* (1936) or the plague of locusts in *The Good Earth* (1937).

He finally conceded that Betty Jaynes and Kenny Baker had no place in this picture, so their roles were written out, thus leaving no Kansas equivalent for the Cowardly Lion. The story had to be tighter, stronger, so all of the love interest was removed. (All that remains of Dorothy's original romance with the farm hand is her fond farewell to the Scarecrow, "I think I'll miss you most of all.") Lizzie Smithers likewise disappeared. *The Wizard of Oz* was slowly moving away from being a conventional musical comedy to being a dramatic film with music. "This picture," LeRoy argued, "does not follow the usual musical comedy formula. We don't have the romance between the handsome tenor and the soprano, nor the clinch for a crescendo finale. We don't need them. Recent productions have proved that."

But, in what Langley believed to be his final shooting script of June 4, he still clung to Mrs. Gulch and her son, Walter, and to the Wicked Witch's attempt to conquer the Emerald City to make Bulbo king. (Here Langley has the Witch finally disclose exactly why she so wants those slippers: "With those shoes I can destroy the Wizard of Oz with three clicks of my heels—as easy as that!—three clicks of my heels!") Now it is explained that the Cowardly Lion is one of the Witch's enchantments: As Dorothy, the Scarecrow, and the Tin Man march through the dark forest, they hear "sinister, invisible voices— about fifteen or twenty, whisper in rhythm to their walk: 'Watch out for the Witch of the West! Watch out for the Witch of the West! . . .' " To break the spell, the Cowardly Lion must fight a real lion in the Witch's castle. She also devises an elaborate plot to get Dorothy's shoes by tricking the girl into falling through a trapdoor into the lion's den; the Witch nonchalantly sacrifices one of her guards when testing her scheme. But it is now Dorothy who kills the

Wicked Witch by dousing her with a bucket of water when the old hag strikes Toto with her broom.

With every improvement, there seemed to be a new problem. Langley wisely provided Dorothy with two trips to the Emerald City as in the book, but the Wizard's escape with her in his balloon is now foiled by a woodpecker. Fortunately the Good Witch arrives to reveal the secret of the magic shoes and sends Dorothy back home. Langley also introduced several clever novelties fully within the spirit of Baum's fairy tale—the cyclone montage, the Horse of a Different Color (originally with "red zebra stripes, purple and green skin"), and the magic crystal in which the image of Aunt Em becomes that of the Wicked Witch. Langley also had Dorothy repeat, "There's no place like home," three times when she clicks her heels together. And he transformed Baum's silver shoes into ruby slippers as a concession to the color photography.

The script also had to keep the score in mind. Langley suggested several likely spots and subjects for songs, such as a "Kansas Song" for Dorothy, "The Wicked Old Witch Is Dead" for the Munchkins, and specialty numbers for the Scarecrow, the Tin Man, and the Cowardly Lion, as well as a "Marching Song" for the girl and her companions. Jerome Kern was the studio's first choice for composer, with lyrics to be provided by either Ira Gershwin or Dorothy Fields, but Kern was just then recovering from a heart attack and a mild stroke and declined to take on so strenuous a job. In the meantime Roger Edens, a musical director at MGM who had worked with Freed on *Broadway Melody of 1936*, attempted several numbers for *The Wizard of Oz*, including "Mid Pleasures and Palaces" for Dorothy in Kansas and a lengthy Munchkinland musical routine. Instead of Edens, Freed suggested that Harold Arlen and Edgar Yipsel ("Yip") Harburg write the music and lyrics for *The Wizard of Oz*, Freed being particularly impressed with their song "In the Shade of the New Apple Tree" in the recent Broadway production *Hooray for What?* (1937).

Arlen and Harburg were hired in early May and given less than four months to provide the complete score for this enormous project. The music was crucial to the development of the story. The producers decided that each song had to be fully integrated with the drama. There would be no stop-action production numbers gratuitously tossed into the action. It was a fairy tale, not a revue. Freed explained, "Music can be a big help properly used as an adjunct and accent to the emotional side of the story, because the masses can feel it." He took as his model *Snow White and the Seven Dwarfs*, in which the love story was defined by the songs, the lyrics arising naturally from Disney's characters and situations. "Dialogue could not have accomplished this half so well," Freed concluded. Perhaps in part due to his great respect for Arlen and Harburg's work, Freed (unlike other producers) ensured the musical integrity of the score by not soliciting numbers from other songwriters to be interpolated into *The Wizard of Oz*.

Arlen and Harburg did not disappoint him. They produced a richly colored and diverse score. They immediately set to work on the lighter, or "lemon-drop," songs, as Arlen called them. The first completed was the jazzy "The Jitterbug," inspired by the swarm of bees sent by the Wicked Witch in Baum's book to destroy Dorothy and her friends. (Evidently no one was concerned that Langley had introduced a similar scene earlier in the script in which the Witch turns the Tin Man into a beehive.) "If I Only Had a Brain . . . a Heart . . . the Nerve" was no more than an old Arlen and Harburg song, "I'm Hanging on to You," cut from *Hooray for What!* with new lyrics for *The Wizard of Oz*. "The Marching Song" became the exuberant "We're Off to See the Wizard," certainly as catchy a tune as the Seven Dwarfs' "Heigh Ho." They also provided a specialty number for Bert Lahr as the Cowardly Lion, "If I Were King of the Forest," a companion to "Song of the Woodman" they had written for him in *The Show Is On* (1936). Arlen and Harburg followed Edens' outline for their elaborate six-minute Munchkinland sequence, combining song and rhymed dialogue in the Gilbert and Sullivan tradition while beautifully integrating contemporary slang (". . . Went flying on her broomstick thumbing for a hitch./And OH, what happened then was rich") with the childlike whimsy of Disney's *The Three Little Pigs* and *Snow White,* concluding with the ebullient "Ding Dong! The Witch Is Dead."*

There were some failed efforts as well. Arlen and Harburg began

---

* Harburg experimented with and then abandoned topical references in his lyrics; for example, the Scarecrow was to sing "And to my darlin' Dor'thy/I'd be Bergen—not McCarthy," the Lion "I could be as good as others/Good enough for Ringling Brothers."

and then abandoned a "Horse of a Different Color" song for the "renovation scene" in favor of transforming Langley's quick musical montage ("Dorothy being dressed in a green dress and having her hair brushed by attendants; then the Tin Man being rubbed and polished till he shines; then the Lion having his mane finger-waved and his coat combed; then the Scarecrow being thumped and patted into shape on a table by two brawny masseurs") into "The Merry Old Land of Oz." They also discarded a "Lions and Tigers and Bears" number, as well as the dirgelike "Death to the Wizard of Oz" when that section of the script was revised. "Off to See the Wizard" was to be reprised still again, up to the gates of the Emerald City, but Arlen and Harburg, with some trimming, came up with the more appropriate but less inspired "Optimistic Voices." Langley also left room for another number in the latter part of the film, "The Wizard's Song," in which Oz

> points out that a heart never made anyone happy, that experience is the only thing that creates a brain, and [that] courage is just the controlling of fear, not the removal of it; while he sings, he goes to a little table that is covered with odds and ends and rubbish; out of a doctor's black bag he takes a little red satin heart and pops it in through a little door in the Tin Man's chest. The Tin Man listens delightedly, then does a little dance of joy at getting his heart. Then the Wizard picks out a large black bottle from the bag, pulls out the cork, and there is a puff of steam out of it and a report. He explains to the Lion that this is Courage. The Lion drinks a mouthful and then gasps, his eyes water and he wheezes, then he goes into his boxer's waltz. Then the Wizard takes a large syringe with Brain-Brightener on it, and sends a shot into the Scarecrow's hat.

A skilled script doctor himself, Harburg wisely decided *not* to set this sequence to music but instead wrote the slyly satirical dialogue himself, thus perfectly defining the humbug Wizard's character, which at best had been shadowy in Langley's script.

The most difficult number to write was Dorothy's Kansas song. Ballads had to stand out from the rest of the score; they were the ones to be singled out as possible hits. Freed demanded a song as lush and emotionally charged as "Someday My Prince Will Come" in

Disney's *Snow White*; Arlen wanted "something with sweep, a melody with a broad, long line." He and Harburg agreed that it should be full of yearning, expressing the child's frustrations living in Kansas. But the melody that Arlen came up with at first seemed inappropriate to Harburg. He thought it beautiful enough, but more suited to Nelson Eddy than to a little girl on the prairie. But Ira Gershwin liked it, and Harburg grew fonder of it the next time he heard it. The bridge, however, had to be simple, childlike, as easy as a finger exercise. Harburg also recognized that the ballad must provide an obvious link between the farm and fairyland; and because the book emphasized the grayness of the prairie, he concluded that the only beauty known to Dorothy was a rainbow. After some false starts, Harburg came up with his song's first line, "Somewhere over the rainbow . . ."

While other elements of the production were showing progress, the script for *The Wizard of Oz* was still unacceptable. On June 3, the day before Langley delivered what he thought was the final draft, LeRoy and Freed brought in the veteran writing team of Florence Ryerson and Edgar Allan Woolf to work on the picture. Woolf was from a prominent New York family (his uncle was the well-known cartoonist Michael Woolf, coincidentally a friend of W. W. Denslow's) and had graduated from Columbia in 1901. His college varsity show became his first play on Broadway, a notorious production but not for his libretto: On the opening night of *Mamzelle Champagne* (1906), at the Madison Square Roof Garden, the millionaire playboy Harry K. Thaw shot and killed the architect Stanford White during the performance in a jealous rage over White's alleged affair with Thaw's wife, the former showgirl Evelyn Nesbit. But Woolf survived this otherwise undistinguished revue to become one of the American theater's most versatile writers, nicknamed "The Tailor of Broadway" for his remarkable ability to do work to order; he had over one hundred vaudeville sketches to his credit as well as several musicals, collaborating with such important composers as Jerome Kern and Sigmund Romberg. He also worked on silent movies and drifted back to Hollywood about 1930, where he wrote several screenplays on his own and contributed uncredited work to others, notably Greta Garbo's scenes in *Grand Hotel* (1932), before teaming with Florence Ryerson.

She was nearly as prolific in her varied career as Woolf in his. Born Florence Willard, she saw her first effort, a fairy play, staged while still in high school. She also sold many short stories to the leading magazines (at least one of hers was illustrated by John R. Neill, who drew the pictures for all of the Oz books except the first), worked on silent movie scripts for Carl Laemmle at Universal, and (with her second husband, Colin Clements) wrote many mystery novels, plays, and dramatic monologues. She began collaborating with Woolf about 1935 and produced several scripts for MGM, including *Everybody Sing* (1938), with Judy Garland, and *Ice Follies of 1939* for LeRoy, before being assigned to *The Wizard of Oz*.

Ryerson and Woolf immediately grasped the relevance of the new film. They noticed that the public's current tastes in movies reflected "a mental retreat which might also be called a stampede back to the simple untroubled hours of childhood." The most popular screen actress of the day was little Shirley Temple; MGM's most lucrative series followed the small-town turmoils of a teenager named Andy Hardy; the success story of the day in Hollywood was an animated children's fantasy, *Snow White and the Seven Dwarfs*. Ryerson and Woolf thought it particularly ironic that "when the drawing of a character in a child's fairy story—Snow White—becomes the number-one heroine of the year, topping the greatest flesh and blood stars in box office appeal, it is time for the adult glamor girls to start worrying." Surely the country was ready for *The Wizard of Oz*. "Perhaps," Ryerson and Woolf observed, "the terrific strain under which we are living—with its war alarms, strikes, horrors at home and abroad that are forced upon us hourly by the radio—has drained life of its old joyousness."

They found Langley's script suffering "a total lack of any real emotion" during Dorothy's adventures in Oz. Arguing that the girl's "desperate desire to get back home should be dramatized more fully," they completely rewrote Langley's screenplay while retaining the basic structure of his adaptation. The motivation of the Wicked Witch also had to be strengthened. They eliminated her plans to conquer the Emerald City to concentrate solely on her obsession with Dorothy's ruby slippers. Consequently Walter and Bulbo were dropped, Mrs. Gulch became single again, and the Witch was given a new companion, a Winged Monkey named Nikko. "We feel that the menace of the Wicked Witch of the West is not used enough," they wrote Freed and LeRoy. "For instance, we should like to see the Witch slinking through the wood whispering to the trees." Even though they did remove Langley's suggestion that the Cowardly Lion be no more than one of her evil enchantments, Ryerson and Woolf bolstered the Witch's role by restoring the Deadly Poppy Field (abandoned by Langley in one of his drafts) as another of her wicked spells. They also rewrote the emotionally charged scene in which Miss Gulch takes Toto away from Dorothy. Ryerson and Woolf, however, strongly objected to the killing of the Wicked Witches as well as that of the Winkie Guard. They advised, "The greatest care should be taken that nothing actually *dies* in the picture, and nothing is too terrifying for children to see." They wanted to soften the blow on the Wicked Witch of the East and have Dorothy quickly pull off the ruby slippers as the Witch "turned into a nice old lady, a parrot, a white tabby cat, or anything else we choose." But fortunately the producers chose otherwise and remained faithful to the book. After all, for nearly forty years, children reading the story had not been terrified by the destroying of Wicked Witches by Dorothy's house and a bucket of water.

Ryerson and Woolf also did not care for Langley's use of the Wizard. Frank Morgan's role in the picture had to be expanded, they argued, so that the audience would not "feel cheated because they didn't see enough of him." They therefore introduced him in the Kansas prologue as "a quaint old medicine man" named Professor Marvel with a midget named Joe and a real lion in a cage, obviously to foreshadow the Munchkins and the Cowardly Lion; he also has a crystal like the Wicked Witch in her castle. They enlarged Morgan's part further by having him also portray the Guardian of the Gate, the Cabby with the Horse of a Different Color, and the Guard to the Wizard's throne room in various disguises and voices.

But Freed was still not happy with the script. He complained that Ryerson and Woolf's version had "no tie-over from Kansas to Oz; there is no conflict, no drama or suspense; Dorothy should be a more imaginative person. . . . Some characters are not funny at all." The greatest problem with the story remained the sequence in the Witch's castle. It was Freed who finally suggested that "Toto should escape and find the rescuers and lead them to Dorothy to rescue her." Obediently Ryerson and Woolf turned Toto into Rin-Tin-Tin in a thrilling race against time reminiscent of the forest animals' pursuit of the Seven Dwarfs when Snow White is poisoned by the Wicked Stepmother. In Ryerson and Woolf's revision, the Wicked Witch now orders the basket containing Toto thrown into the river, but the little dog swims to safety and runs to get the Scarecrow, Tin Man, and Cowardly Lion to free Dorothy. "The whole feeling of this scene," they noted, "should be continuous movement, like the Northwest Mounted going to the rescue."

Ryerson and Woolf did tighten and thus strengthen the action of the story, but they created as many new problems as they solved. Their most elaborate contribution to the drama was a Rainbow Bridge created by the Wicked Witch to send Dorothy to her death, much like Langley's trapdoor. This marvelous special effect, introduced to test the possibilities of double exposure on Technicolor film, is suggested to the Wicked Witch by a reprise of "Over the Rainbow" in a scene similar to one in Disney's *Snow White.* Just as the Wicked Stepmother turned Snow White into a scullery maid, the Witch orders Dorothy to mop the castle floor, and while sitting by a fountain, the girl sings "Over the Rainbow," "putting all her heart and soul into her song," as the audience now realizes "that the lovely land over the rainbow for which she yearns is no longer a foreign land but Kansas—the farm—*home.*" The Witch then brews a thin Rainbow Bridge and tricks Dorothy into running across it to her friends. But instead of her falling through, the ruby slippers carry the girl across to their loving arms.

In enlarging the Wicked Witch's part, Ryerson and Woolf were obligated to do the same with the Good Witch's role. The "plump, kindly, cheerful little" Good Witch of the North merged into the beautiful Good Witch of the South of Baum's story, as she evolved into Dorothy's fairy godmother in Oz. Now named Glinda from the book, she unexpectedly reappears when Dorothy melts the Wicked Witch, to inform the girl, "The broomstick, Dorothy—the broomstick will take you to Oz." And to the strains of a reprise of "Ding Dong! The Witch Is Dead," "against the full moon, the four of them —Dorothy, with Toto in her arms, the Scarecrow, the Tin Man, and the Lion—can be seen, all riding on the broomstick."

Ryerson and Woolf made other unnecessary changes. Back at the

Emerald City Dorothy unmasks the Wizard before his own people, who then force him and Dorothy and her companions to flee in the balloon. Langley's woodpecker reappears and bursts the balloon, sending them plummeting to Dorothy's cries, "Oh, Glinda—dear Glinda—please save us!" The Good Witch then directs "the whole miniature Munchkin Fire Department" to catch them in a huge net. Dorothy has landed back where she began, and the ruby slippers now take the child *and* her house back to Kansas. Once the dream is over, she is reunited with her friends on the farm, including Professor Marvel, and the camera pans to his mangy lion in the cage, dissolving to MGM's Leo the Lion logo.

Although conceding that Ryerson and Woolf added considerably to the script, Freed nevertheless still preferred much of Langley's work. He was particularly insistent that Dorothy repeat, "There's no place like home," three times when clicking her heels together. He found Ryerson and Woolf's dialogue in spots "too long and a bit precious" while praising Langley's for its "crispness." Other sections seemed pointless or padded, the characters too melodramatic in places. Evidently Freed believed he had gone as far as he could with Ryerson and Woolf and took them off *The Wizard of Oz* on July 27 to work on his new picture, *Babes in Arms* (1939). "I think," Freed noted, "we should go through the whole script with the thought in mind of using the minimum of dialogue and that Langley would be of great help on this in getting a rhythm through the whole script in one flavor of writing."

But when Langley returned on July 30, he was furious that other writers had tampered with his screenplay. He ripped into their manuscript, taking out great sections and replacing them with his own. He even restored his Deadly Poppy Field scene dropped from an earlier draft; he thought his snowstorm more dramatic than Ryerson and Woolf's awakening Dorothy with the Tin Man's tears, a conceit they had taken from such traditional fairy tales as "The Sleeping Beauty" and "Snow White." Langley also convinced the studio that the Rainbow Bridge sequence was not only pointless but far too expensive to film.*

---

* See Appendix E, pp. 144–151. The studio may have also decided to drop the Rainbow Bridge when a representative of one of the owners of the old Baum musical comedy *The Tik-Tok Man of Oz* claimed that it had been taken from this earlier play.

But the producers liked much of Ryerson and Woolf's revision. The movie was scheduled to go into production in mid-September, and still there was no script. Although he received no screen credit for his considerable contribution to the screenplay, Harburg was brought in to work out a compromise from the various drafts. While preferring Langley's version, Harburg had also worked congenially with Ryerson and Woolf during their tenure on the film and saw some value in many of their decisions. Harburg's revision, therefore, was a judicious blending of Langley with Ryerson and Woolf as well as additional dialogue of his own. Then, between August 3 and September 2, another writer, Jack Mintz, was assigned to provide further gags for the Scarecrow, Tin Man, and Cowardly Lion.

The date of the studio's official "final shooting script" is October 8, but even that varies considerably from the completed film. The shifting of directors required further changes in screenwriters. The first to be considered was Norman Taurog, who had won his Oscar guiding Jackie Cooper through *Skippy* (1931), but he was soon reassigned to *The Adventures of Huckleberry Finn* (1938) with Mickey Rooney. He was succeeded on *The Wizard of Oz* by Richard Thorpe, responsible for several Tarzan pictures for MGM. He brought in comic Sid Silvers (who had worked on *Broadway Melody of 1936* and *Born to Dance,* 1936) to help with script revisions when needed. Then Thorpe took over *Huckleberry Finn* from Taurog, and Silvers lasted on *The Wizard of Oz* as long as Thorpe did—until October 22. George Cukor, who had already brought to the screen such literary classics as *Little Women* (1933) and *David Copperfield* (1935), was director of the picture for only seven days before he left to begin *Gone With the Wind* (1939). Finally Victor Fleming took on *The Wizard of Oz.* He had previously filmed other children's books, *Treasure Island* (1934) and *Captains Courageous* (1937), as well as recently helped (although uncredited) with *The Good Earth* (1937). If anyone on the MGM lot could tame the mammoth musical, it was Fleming. He immediately requested John Lee Mahin, with whom he had collaborated on *Treasure Island, Captains Courageous,* and other projects, to help smooth over the rough spots in the script during the shooting.

Mahin's official time with *The Wizard of Oz* ran from October 27, 1938, to January 10, 1939, but he actually stayed on the picture as long as Fleming did. Changes in the dialogue were frequent and sometimes made on the day of the shooting of a particular scene. Some were not even written down, while others were obviously ad-libbed by the cast. And Mahin was not the only or the last one revising the script. Just a few days before Christmas, Fleming demanded additional lyrics and music for the end of the Munchkinland sequence, and Harburg and Arlen immediately wrote "Follow the Yellow Brick Road" to lead into "We're Off to See the Wizard." Langley, too, was writing new scenes as late as March 3.

The most significant revisions of this "final shooting script," however, were Mahin's. He wrote an entirely new opening to the Kansas prologue, defining Dorothy's character by making her the predominant character from the first shot. He added a third farm hand, named Zeke, to become the Cowardly Lion in Oz. This last change necessitated the dropping of Professor Marvel's lion, and Joe the dwarf was replaced by a horse named Sylvester. It was Mahin who introduced Toto's chasing of Miss Gulch's cat, which provided a perfect way of foreshadowing the dog's jumping out of the Wizard's balloon to catch another cat in the Emerald City and thus eliminated all the nonsense with the woodpecker. Also in the prologue Mahin greatly softened Aunt Em's character; in previous drafts it was not always clear whether it was she or Miss Gulch who was the Wicked Witch of the West. ("Her an' a snappin' turtle was hatched from the same egg," Hickory says about the farm woman in Ryerson and Woolf's script.) Despite Mahin's efforts, Aunt Em as played by Clara Blandick remained uncomfortably waspish.* All that was left of Dorothy's rescue from the Wicked Witch was a chase through the castle and the inevitable melting; and the discovery of Oz the Terrible generally followed Baum's story with the exception that now Glinda suddenly appears once the Wizard is lost in his balloon to reveal the secret of the ruby slippers. In the end most of the troubles with the

---

* The mellowing of Aunt Em continued as late as the final shooting, when some of Mahin's lines were cut. Uncle Henry regrets that his poor orphan niece is troubled by Miss Gulch and that the girl has no playmates, but Aunt Em callously comments, "I know—but we all got to work out our own problems, Henry." Dorothy tells Professor Marvel that no one cares for her at home, that "Auntie Em was going to let them kill Toto." When she is just about convinced to return home, Dorothy has second thoughts. "If I go home," she says to Toto, "they'll send you to the Sheriff! If I don't—Aunt Em may—why, she may *die!*" So Dorothy must choose between her aunt and her dog. But she quickly comes up with a solution: "I know! I'll give you to Hunk. He'll watch out for you!" If only she had thought of that before. . . .

script were easily resolved by simply going back to what L. Frank Baum had done in *The Wonderful Wizard of Oz.*

Mahin also had to punch up the comedy in the picture, particularly for Bert Lahr, and relied on Jack Haley, who, a former vaudevillian like both Lahr and Ray Bolger, supplied some old gags. "Come on, Jack, let's have some jokes," Mahin asked the Tin Man. "And we'll turn them into Frank Baum language so poor Frank won't roll in his grave." (A good number of these were eventually cut from the final film.) Surprisingly Mahin did not demand screen credit for his crucial reworking of the script; he admitted that the basic structure and most of the dialogue of the final film were already there before Fleming brought him in, so his surgery was merely cosmetic. No matter how many writers finally had a hand in its writing, the credits on the screen state simply "Screen Play by Noel Langley, Florence Ryerson and Edgar Allan Woolf. Adaptation by Noel Langley."

Although Victor Fleming was given sole screen credit for the direction of *The Wizard of Oz,* he did not actually complete it. Three weeks away from wrapping up the picture, Fleming was called by David O. Selznick to take over *Gone With the Wind* from Cukor. Because the studio was distributing the film for Selznick, MGM approved the change and replaced Fleming with King Vidor, known for such dramas as *The Big Parade* (1925) and *The Crowd* (1928) rather than for musicals. All that was left for him to do on the picture was to shoot the Kansas scenes (and reshoot some Technicolor footage), and it was appropriate that the framing sequences be in a style distinctive from the adventures in Oz. He completed principal photography of *The Wizard of Oz* by mid-March.

Fleming, however, returned to aid in the editing of the picture late into the night after his work on *Gone With the Wind* was finished for the day. Bits of dialogue and other business actually filmed were snipped as the rough cut was rushed into shape for a sneak preview in late June. The studio was favorably impressed with the movie, but it still needed work before it could be released to the theaters. Some small children attending the screening were so terrified by the Wicked Witch that they had to be taken out of the theater. Judiciously the studio edited out some of her menacing lines.

It was also too long. They excised most of the Scarecrow's dance as well as a scene in which the Wicked Witch actually turns the Tin Man into a beehive. But the more radical cuts involved two of the most expensive sequences to stage. The elaborate reprise of "Ding Dong! The Witch Is Dead," described as the "triumphant procession" in which Dorothy and her friends jubilantly parade through the Emerald City with the Witch's broomstick, had to go. It may have taken five weeks and $80,000 to film "The Jitterbug," but that number, too, was cut.* The song did not add materially to the progress of the story and slowed down the picture. It was also feared that being associated with the recent jitterbug dance craze might "date" the movie for future releases. (When LeRoy explained that the picture might be good for at least ten years, Margaret Hamilton told him, "You're crazy!") Unfortunately, in dropping the scene, no one thought of editing out of the final print the Witch's remark to the Winged Monkeys, "I've sent a little insect on ahead to take the fight out of them." The removal of both "The Jitterbug" and the "triumphant procession" now made *The Wizard of Oz* a musical in which the last third of the film has no music. "Over the Rainbow" might also have ended up on the cutting room floor (the studio executives could not see why Dorothy was singing in a barnyard) had not Freed fought to keep it in the picture.

The official "world premiere" of the film was on August 12, 1939, at the Strand Theatre in Oconomowoc, Wisconsin, followed by the gala premiere at Grauman's Chinese Theatre in Hollywood on August 15, and its Broadway opening at Loew's Capitol Theatre on August 17, featuring a special appearance of Judy Garland and Mickey Rooney on stage. While the more sophisticated journals, such as *The New Yorker* and *The New Republic,* panned it and *The Harvard Lampoon* named it one of the *worst* pictures of the year, most of the other reviewers found much to praise in *The Wizard of Oz*; Damon Runyan went so far as to call it "one of the greatest pictures we have ever viewed." Of course even the raves contained some reservations (it is now remarkable that some of the critics did

---

* Judy Garland did record "The Jitterbug" for the Decca album of songs from the movie; Betty Hutton also released it as a single. The tune is similar to that of Richard Rodgers's "Bali Ha'i" from *South Pacific* (1949), but Arlen said he did not mind when it ended up in so beautiful a song as that.

not care for the Arlen-Harburg score), but the audiences, both young and old, loved the movie.

But why after fifty years should *The Wizard of Oz* remain one of the most popular pictures in motion picture history? In the curtain speech L. Frank Baum delivered on the opening night of his musical back in 1902, he likened the creation of this early stage production to the making of a plum pudding: He, as the author, may have provided the flour, but the composer brought the spice, the actors the plums, everyone else something flavorful of his own, the whole of which was beaten into shape by the master chef, the director. This metaphor is equally apt in describing the 1939 movie. Everyone involved added some crucial ingredient to this marvelous confection. Harold Arlen and E. Y. Harburg provided one of the most tuneful of all original film scores. Arnold Gillespie's numerous special effects still hold their magic after all these years. Victor Fleming's no-nonsense direction ultimately keeps the fantasy from getting out of hand. Cedric Gibbons' art direction and Adrian's fanciful costumes retain their distinctive charm. Little details of contemporary taste and style (such as Dorothy's anklets and the Optimistic Voices that sound like the Boswell sisters) that threaten to date the film are fortunately few. There are no airplanes, not even an automobile, and few reminders of the Great Depression in this American fairy tale.

Much of the credit for the picture's perpetual youth must also go to the performances. Each seems to slip so effortlessly into his or her bizarre costume that none was ever fully to shake off the spell of this motion picture. Ray Bolger will always be the Scarecrow, Jack Haley the Tin Man, Bert Lahr the Cowardly Lion, and Margaret Hamilton the Wicked Witch of the West. And certainly the fantasy would not work without Judy Garland's Dorothy.

And one should not forget the script of *The Wizard of Oz.* Yes, it does wander off from Baum's Yellow Brick Road from time to time, but never completely away from the spirit of the children's book. It is a shame that Hollywood compromised and turned Dorothy's journey to the Land of Oz into merely a dream. (The plot risks losing its perspective in the Deadly Poppy Field: Does Dorothy have a dream within her dream when she falls asleep among the poisonous blossoms?) Some of the most memorable lines ("Toto, I've a feeling we're not in Kansas anymore"; "Lions and tigers and bears—Oh my!") are

Noel Langley's, while Florence Ryerson and Edgar Allan Woolf provided Arthur Freed's "real assault on our hearts." And one should not underestimate E. Y. Harburg's, John Lee Mahin's, and Victor Fleming's contributions to the shaping of the narrative. Still, no matter how many people finally struggled with the script, the movie of *The Wizard of Oz* remains Baum's story.

No final screenplay of *The Wizard of Oz* survives—if indeed there was one. Many drafts, from Herman J. Mankiewicz to John Lee Mahin, do exist, including the official shooting script of October 7, 1938, but even that contains revisions dated as late as February 28, 1939, some of which do not conform to the released film. Other changes were not even written down, being made on set or in the cutting room. The studio did prepare a continuity script of the rough cut of the film on March 15; this version contains the principal scenes (the Scarecrow's dance; the beehive; "The Jitterbug"; and the "triumphant procession") that were edited out of the final print. These are included for the first time here in the appendices. Another sequence, describing the Rainbow Bridge, taken from Ryerson and Woolf's last draft, is also published in the back. Another continuity script, recording every shot, action, and line of dialogue taken directly from the film itself, which was pulled together by the studio for copyright purposes, has also survived. The text of this book is principally the official shooting script, checked against the final continuity script and the motion picture itself. Therefore here, for the first time, is printed every word of the classic movie, up to "Oh, Auntie Em, there's no place like home!" What the film said of Baum's story in its dedication a half-century ago is equally true of the picture itself. And surely *The Wizard of Oz* will survive another fifty years. . . .

THE WIZARD OF OZ:
THE SCREENPLAY

FADE IN:

FADE OUT:
(LION ROAR)

FADE IN:

Metro-Goldwyn-Mayer
Presents

LAP DISSOLVE TO:

"THE
WIZARD
OF OZ"

Copyright MCMXXXIX in U. S. A.
By Loew's Incorporated
All Rights in the Motion Picture
Reserved Under International Conventions
Passed by the National Board of Review Ars Gratia Artis
A Metro-Goldwyn-Mayer Picture
(Trade Mark)
Produced by
Loew's Incorporated

LAP DISSOLVE TO:

A
VICTOR FLEMING
PRODUCTION

LAP DISSOLVE TO:

with
JUDY GARLAND
FRANK MORGAN

RAY BOLGER
BERT LAHR
JACK HALEY
BILLIE BURKE
MARGARET HAMILTON
CHARLEY GRAPEWIN
AND THE MUNCHKINS

LAP DISSOLVE TO:

Screen Play by
NOEL LANGLEY,
FLORENCE RYERSON,
and EDGAR ALLAN WOOLF

Adaptation by
NOEL LANGLEY

From the Book by
L. FRANK BAUM

LAP DISSOLVE TO:

MUSICAL PROGRAM

Musical Adaptation by
HERBERT STOTHART

Lyrics by	*Music by*
E. Y. HARBURG	HAROLD ARLEN

Associate Conductor . . . . GEORGE STOLL

Orchestral and Vocal
Arrangements . . . . GEORGE BASSMAN
MURRAY CUTTER
PAUL MARQUARDT
KEN DARBY

Musical Numbers Staged by BOBBY CONNOLLY

LAP DISSOLVE TO:

Photographed in Technicolor

Photographed in
   Technicolor by . . . . HAROLD ROSSON, A.S.C.
Associate . . . . ALLEN DAVEY, A.S.C.
Technicolor Color Director . . . . . . NATALIE KALMUS
Associate . . . . HENRI JAFFA

   LAP DISSOLVE TO:

Recording Director . . . . DOUGLAS SHEARER
Art Director . . . . CEDRIC GIBBONS
   Associate . . . . WILLIAM A. HORNING
   Set Decorations . . . . EDWIN B. WILLIS
Special Effects . . . . ARNOLD GILLESPIE
Costumes by . . . . ADRIAN
Character Make-Ups
   Created by . . . . JACK DAWN
Film Editor . . . . BLANCHE SEWELL

Western Electric SOUND SYSTEM
(Trade Mark)

M.P.P.D.A. Seal   I.A.T.S.E.
Certificate No. 5364   Insignia

   LAP DISSOLVE TO:

                  Produced by
                  MERVYN LeROY

   LAP DISSOLVE TO:

                  Directed by
                 VICTOR FLEMING

   LAP DISSOLVE TO:

FADE IN:

For nearly forty years this story has given faithful service to the Young in Heart; and Time has been powerless to put its kindly philosophy out of fashion.

To those of you who have been faithful to it in return

. . . and to the Young in Heart—we dedicate this picture.

FADE OUT:

FADE IN:
LONG SHOT—COUNTRY ROAD—DAY

From the foreground a long straight road leads to and past the farm. Into the shot, from past CAMERA, half running and half walking backward, comes DOROTHY, a little girl of twelve, and her dog, TOTO. She stops a moment, and looks down the road in the direction from which she came. She seems a little breathless and apprehensive.

MEDIUM SHOT—DOROTHY

DOROTHY *(to* TOTO*)* She isn't coming yet, Toto . . .
(kneeling down and examining him)
Did she hurt you? She tried to, didn't she?
(rising as she picks up books and starts along road toward home)
Come on—we'll go tell Uncle Henry and Auntie Em . . . Come on, Toto!

LONG SHOT—GALE FARM—PORCH AND SIDE YARD

DOROTHY comes running in the gate from the road and around to the side of the house where AUNT EM and UNCLE HENRY are working with an old coal-oil five-hundred-chick incubator.

DOROTHY *(as she runs)* Aunt—Em—! Aunt—Em—!

THREE SHOT—AUNT EM, UNCLE HENRY, AND DOROTHY

UNCLE HENRY and AUNT EM with worried faces are taking small live chicks from the incubator, putting them quickly under clucking, broody hens, which are nearby in crates. They count to themselves as DOROTHY runs into scene. AUNT EM wears a cooking apron.

DOROTHY   Aunt—Em—!

AUNT EM *(putting live chicks into her apron)*   Sixty-seven, sixty-eight—

DOROTHY *(breathless)*   Just listen to what Miss Gulch did to Toto! She—

AUNT EM   Dorothy—*please*—we're trying to count! Sixty-eight . . .

DOROTHY   Oh, but Aunt Em, she hit him over the—

UNCLE HENRY   Don't bother us now, honey. This old incubator's gone bad, and we're likely to lose a lot of our chicks.

DOROTHY *(picking up a chick)*   Oh—oh, the poor little things . . .
(then back to the subject of TOTO *again)*
Oh, but Aunt Em—Miss Gulch hit Toto right over the back with a rake—just because she says he gets in her garden and chases her nasty old cat every day!

AUNT EM *(taking* DOROTHY'S *chick to put under a hen)*   Seventy—
(then more exasperated)
Dorothy, *please!*

DOROTHY   Oh, but he doesn't do it every day—just once or twice a week—and he can't catch her old cat anyway. And now she says she's going to get the Sheriff—and—

AUNT EM   Dorothy, Dorothy—*we're busy!*

DOROTHY *(mournfully)*   Oh, all right.
(She walks offscreen, toward the barnyard.)

MEDIUM SHOT—BACK OF HOUSE—BARNYARD

ZEKE, HUNK, and HICKORY, farm hands, are busy straining to lift the body of a large wagon onto the wheels. It has been patched up with old boards, etc. DOROTHY enters the scene.

ZEKE   How's she coming?

HUNK   Take it easy. Ow!—you got my finger!

ZEKE   Well, why don't you get your finger out of the way?

HICKORY   There you are.

HUNK   Right on my finger!

ZEKE   It's a lucky thing it wasn't your head.

DOROTHY   Zeke, what am I going to do about Miss Gulch? Just because Toto chases her old cat—

ZEKE   *(hurrying away)*   Listen, honey—I got them hogs to get in.

He hurries away, followed by HICKORY. HUNK takes up a hammer to drive in a bolt.

HUNK   Now lookit, Dorothy—you ain't using your head about Miss Gulch. Think you didn't have any brains at all!

DOROTHY   I have *so* got brains!

HUNK   Well, why don't you use 'em! When you come home, don't go by Miss Gulch's place. Then Toto won't get in her garden, and you won't get in no trouble, see?

DOROTHY   *(knowing he's right but not willing to admit it because of his patronizing attitude)*   Oh, Hunk—you just won't listen, that's all. *(She goes away toward ZEKE offscreen.)*

HUNK   *(calling after her as he hammers)*   Well, your head ain't made of straw, you know!
(On this, not looking at what he is doing, he hammers his injured finger again.)
Ow!* *(whirling around)*

---

* At this point in the film was another scene (deleted from the final cut), concerning Hickory's "contraption" that Aunt Em refers to later in the prologue and which foreshadows his reappearance as the Tin Man:

TWO SHOT—HICKORY AND DOROTHY

As DOROTHY *enters scene,* HICKORY *is working on his wind machine—a strange contraption of an old boiler, funnel, wires tubes, etc., connecting to a small rattle-trap motor.*

LONG SHOT—ZEKE AT STY GATE

He is calling hogs as they come in past CAMERA from the yard. In the background DOROTHY approaches him from behind and climbs up on the fence, walking on it and balancing herself.

ZEKE Soo-eee! *(shooing in a wayward hog)* Get in there before I make a dime bank outa ya! *(pouring feed in trough)* Listen, kid—are you going to let that old Gulch heifer try and buffalo ya? She ain't nothing to be afraid of. Have a little courage, that's all.

DOROTHY I'm not afraid of her.

ZEKE Then the next time she squawks, walk right up to her and spit in her eye. That's what I'd do.

DOROTHY *(tottering with a scream)* Oh!
(She falls into pen.)
Oh! Oh, Zeke! Help! Help me, Zeke, get me out of here! Help! Oh! Oh!

ZEKE is over the fence like lightning, takes DOROTHY's foot out of a wire, and carries her out over the pen. He jumps out as HICKORY and HUNK come running, sits down, and begins wiping his brow.

HICKORY Are you all right, Dorothy?

HICKORY *(straightening up)* Oh! Oh, it feels like my joints are rusted. Listen, Dorothy, don't let Hunk kid you about Miss Gulch. She's just a poor sour-faced old maid that—she ain't got no heart left. You know, you should have a little more heart yourself, and have pity on her.

DOROTHY *(morosely)* Well, gee—I try and have a little heart—

HICKORY Now look here—here's something that really has a heart. This is the best invention I ever invented.

DOROTHY *(not very interested)* This?

HICKORY Sure. It's to break up winds, so we don't have no more dust storms. Can you imagine what it'll mean to this section of the country. I'll show you. It works perfect now. *(As he says this, he switches on the motor. An open pet-cock or valve shoots a stream of oil into his eyes as he bends over.)*
Here's the principle. You see that fan—that sends up air currents—Oh, stop it!

DOROTHY Oh!

HICKORY Who did it? Now wait a minute.

DOROTHY *(disgusted, moving away)* Hickory!

HICKORY Now what happened? I'll bet Hunk did it.

DOROTHY *(shaken)* Yes, I'm all right. Oh, I fell in and—and
Zeke—
(looking at ZEKE, *who is shaking and wiping his head with his
handkerchief—she laughs)*
Why, Zeke—you're just as scared as I am!

HUNK *(laughing at* ZEKE *with* HICKORY) What's the matter?
Gonna let a little old pig make a coward out of ya?

HICKORY Look at you, Zeke—you're just as white—

At this point, AUNT EM comes up carrying a bowl of crullers.

AUNT EM Here—here—what's all this jabber-wapping when there's
work to be done! I know three shiftless farm hands that'll be out of
a job before they know it.

HICKORY *(trying to explain)* Well, Dorothy was walking along—

AUNT EM I saw you tinkering with that contraption, Hickory! Now
you and Hunk get back to that wagon.

HICKORY *(shaking his finger in the air)* All right, Mrs. Gale—but
someday they're going to erect a statue to me in this town, and—

AUNT EM Well, don't start posing for it now!

HUNK laughs at him.

AUNT EM Here—here—can't work on an empty stomach. Have
some crullers.

HUNK *(as she passes them around)* Gosh, Mrs. Gale!

HICKORY *(taking some)* Oh, thanks.

AUNT EM Just fried.

HUNK Swell!

HICKORY and HUNK dart off.

ZEKE *(trying to explain, as he takes a cruller)* You see—Dorothy
toppled in with the big Duroc—

AUNT EM It's no place for Dorothy around a pigsty! Now, you go feed those hogs before they worry themselves into anemia!

ZEKE *(exiting)* Yes'm.

AUNT EM starts back toward the house, as DOROTHY takes a cruller and follows her. We TRUCK WITH THEM.

DOROTHY Auntie Em—really—you know what Miss Gulch said she was going to do to Toto? She said she was gonna—

AUNT EM Now, Dorothy dear—stop imagining things . . . you always get yourself into a fret over nothing.

DOROTHY No—

AUNT EM Now, you just help us out today and find yourself a place where you won't get into any trouble!

AUNT EM goes on as we HOLD and DOROTHY stands looking sadly after her, munching her cruller. She looks down at TOTO.

DOROTHY Someplace where there isn't any trouble . . .
(tossing a piece to TOTO)
. . . do you suppose there is such a place, Toto?
(dreamily to herself)
There must be. It's not a place you can get to by a boat or a train. It's far, far away . . .
(music starts)
Behind the moon
Beyond the rain
(singing)
Somewhere, over the rainbow, way up high,
There's a land that I heard of once in a lullaby.

Somewhere, over the rainbow, skies are blue,
And the dreams that you dare to dream really do
come true.

Someday I'll wish upon a star
And wake up where the clouds are far behind me,
Where troubles melt like lemon drops,

Away above the chimney tops
That's where you'll find me.*

Somewhere over the rainbow, bluebirds fly,
Birds fly over the rainbow,
Why then, oh why can't I?

SHOT OF SUN RAYS THROUGH CLOUDS

DOROTHY *(singing)*
If happy little bluebirds fly
Beyond the rainbow,
Why oh why can't I?

LONG SHOT—THE ROADWAY—APPROACHING THE FARM

This is a narrow little lane. A bicycle is pedaling along with MISS GULCH sitting stiffly on the seat. There is a basket strapped to the back of the 'cycle. A rolled umbrella is fastened to the handlebar.

The CAMERA follows her as she reaches the gate to the farmhouse. UNCLE HENRY is painting the fence.

MISS GULCH *(as she gets off bicycle and takes basket from rear)*   Mr. Gale!

UNCLE HENRY *(without any enthusiasm, as he opens the swinging gate for her)*   Howdy, Miss Gulch.

MISS GULCH *(sharply)*   I want to see you and your wife right away about Dorothy.

UNCLE HENRY *(worried)*   Dorothy? Well, what has Dorothy done?

MISS GULCH *(indignantly)*   What's she done? I'm all but lame from the bite on my leg!

UNCLE HENRY   You mean she bit ya?

---

* This lyric to the bridge differs from the original in the shooting script:
Someday I'll wake and rub my eyes
And in that land beyond the skies you'll find me
I'll be a laughin' daffodil
And leave the silly cares that fill my mind behind me . . .
The final tag was added at the time of the scene's filming.

MISS GULCH   No, her dog!

UNCLE HENRY   Oh, she bit her dog, eh?

He drops his hold on the gate, which swings closed and gives MISS GULCH a smart little spank.

MISS GULCH *(after the gate hits her)*   No!

LAP DISSOLVE TO:
INT. GALE SITTING ROOM
It is a typical old-fashioned farmhouse parlor. Flowered wallpaper, family pictures on the wall, plush furniture, etc. etc.

AUNT EM and MISS GULCH are seated as DOROTHY enters with TOTO in her arms. In the background UNCLE HENRY is looking very unhappy.

MISS GULCH *(to AUNT EM)*   That dog's a menace to the community. I'm taking him to the Sheriff and make sure he's destroyed.

DOROTHY   Destroyed? Toto? Oh, you can't . . . you mustn't . . . Auntie Em—Uncle Henry—you won't let her . . . will you?

UNCLE HENRY   Uh . . . ah . . . course, we won't . . . eh . . . a . . .
(his voice breaking a little, uncertain, as he looks at his wife)
Will we, Em?

DOROTHY   Please, Aunt Em! Toto didn't mean to. He didn't know he was doing anything wrong. I'm the one that ought to be punished. I let him go in her garden . . . you can send me to bed without supper—

MISS GULCH *(angrily, to AUNT EM)*   If you don't hand over that dog, I'll bring a damage suit that'll take your whole farm! There's a law protectin' folks against dogs that bite!

AUNT EM *(to MISS GULCH, dryly)*   How would it be if she keeps him tied up? He's really gentle—with gentle people, that is.

MISS GULCH   Well, that's for the Sheriff to decide—
(producing a paper for AUNT EM)
—here's his order allowing me to take him—

(warningly)
—unless you want to go against the law.

UNCLE HENRY *(looking at order)* Uh—yeah—

AUNT EM We can't go against the law, Dorothy.
(It is plain that she is struggling to hide some emotion.)
I'm afraid poor Toto will have to go.

MISS GULCH Now you're seeing reason.

DOROTHY No—

MISS GULCH *(producing basket)* Here's what I'm taking him in so
he can't attack me again!

DOROTHY *(going suddenly berserk as she sees* MISS GULCH *coming
toward her)* Oh, no—no—I won't let you take him. You go away
you—ooh—I'll bite you myself!

AUNT EM Dorothy!

DOROTHY *(wildly)* You wicked old witch! Uncle Henry, Auntie Em!
Don't let 'em take Toto! Don't let her take him—please!

MISS GULCH I've got a notice! Let me have him!

DOROTHY Stop her!

AUNT EM *(almost unable to speak)* Put him in the basket, Henry.

HENRY, *very reluctantly, puts* TOTO *in the basket* MISS GULCH
is holding.

MISS GULCH The idea!

DOROTHY Oh, don't, Uncle Henry. Oh, Toto! Don't . . .

*With an expression of utter despair, she runs out of the room, sob-
bing. AUNT EM stands looking at MISS GULCH with an expression of repressed anger.*

AUNT EM Almira Gulch . . . just because you own half the
county doesn't mean you have the power to run the rest of us! For
twenty-three years I've been dying to tell you what I thought of

you . . . and now . . . well—being a Christian woman—I can't say it!

She, too, runs off as UNCLE HENRY sits down, chuckling, with MISS GULCH aghast at what she has heard.

DISSOLVE TO:
EXTERIOR ROADWAY—CLOSE ON MISS GULCH

MISS GULCH is pedaling along, the basket strapped to the rear of the bicycle. The lid is bumping up and down, straining the catch.

TOTO manages to work the catch loose. He scrambles out of the basket. The CAMERA PANS to show him streaking back toward the farm.

QUICK LAP TO:
INT. DOROTHY'S ROOM
On the night table is a picture of DOROTHY and AUNT EM standing at the farm gate.

DOROTHY is sitting on the floor by TOTO's bed, still crying. TOTO barks as he hurtles through the open window in one wild leap and lands on the bed.

DOROTHY   Toto! Darling! Oh, I got you back! You came back! Oh, I'm so glad! Toto!
(She hugs him happily for a moment, then suddenly realizes their danger.)
Oh, they'll be coming back for you in a minute. We've got to get away!
(She holds him close and then pulls an ancient straw bag out from under the bed.)
We've got to run away!

LAP DISSOLVE TO:
EXTREME CLOSE ON A DUSTY ROAD

This is shooting straight down and gets two rows of rather pathetic little footprints . . . one set made by DOROTHY, one by TOTO. The SOUNDTRACK carries music that suggests weariness. MOVE CAMERA ALONG to get the feet that are making the prints.

DOROTHY is going down the road with her bag and basket. TOTO is trotting a bit to one side. The two look very small and forlorn against the immensity of the prairie, which spreads out in every direction.

LAP DISSOLVE TO:
LONG SHOT—BRIDGE AND GULLY

The same figures are just passing across a bridge. In the foreground is a little gully. Beside it is a decorated wagon—all very dusty and shabby. Humming of a voice comes over scene as DOROTHY reads the large lettering on the wagon:

PROFESSOR

MARVEL

ACCLAIMED BY

The CROWNED HEADS of EUROPE

LET HIM   IN HIS

READ YOUR PAST PRESENT and FUTURE CRYSTAL

ALSO JUGGLING AND SLEIGHT of HAND

To the side of the entrance reads: BALLOON EXHIBITIONIST. The humming voice is coming from a man we shall know as PROFESSOR MARVEL, an old carnival fakir, who steps down out of the wagon and walks over to the fire.

PROFESSOR MARVEL   Well—well—well! Houseguests, huh? Ha, ha, ha, ha! And who might you be? Heh!
(before DOROTHY *starts to answer)*
No, no, no, now don't tell me!
(He puts his hand to his brow like a mind reader. When he speaks, it is in the typical patter of a sideshow fakir. He sits down and picks up toasting fork.)
Let's see . . . you're . . . you're traveling in disguise—No! that's not right . . . I . . . you're . . . you're going on a visit— No! I'm wrong . . . that's . . . you're . . . you're . . . *running away!*

DOROTHY   How did you guess?

PROFESSOR MARVEL Ha, ha! Professor Marvel never guesses—he *knows!* Heh, heh! Now *why* are you running away?

DOROTHY Why . . .

PROFESSOR MARVEL No, no, now don't tell me. They . . . they don't understand you at home. They don't appreciate you . . . you want to see other lands—big cities—big mountains—big oceans . . . heh!

DOROTHY *(in awed tones)* Why, it's just like you could read what was inside of me.

PROFESSOR MARVEL *(laughs)* Ye-heh—

TOTO runs forward and grabs a wienie off of the PROFESSOR's fork.

DOROTHY Oh, Toto! That's not polite! We haven't been asked yet!

PROFESSOR MARVEL Ha, ha, ha! He's perfectly welcome! Heh, heh! As one dog to another, huh? *(puts another wienie on the fork)* Ha, ha, ha, ha! Here now . . . let's see . . . where were we?

DOROTHY *(remembering the sign)* Oh, please, Professor, why can't we go with you and see all the crowned heads of Europe?

PROFESSOR MARVEL Do you know any? *(suddenly remembering the sign)* Oh, you mean the thing, yes . . . Well, I . . . I never do anything without consulting my crystal first. *(rising)* Let's go inside here. We'll . . . just come along. I'll show you . . . *(He leads her into the wagon.)*

INT. WAGON

DOROTHY and the PROFESSOR enter. The wagon is fitted up with the usual hocus-pocus, such as a fortune-telling booth. The PROFESSOR seats DOROTHY as he dons a headdress and lights two candles on both sides of his chair and sits opposite her.

PROFESSOR MARVEL That's right. Here, sit right down here. That's it. Heh, heh! *(indicating crystal)* This . . . this is the same, genuine, magic, authentic crystal used by the priests of Isis and Osiris in the days of the Pharaohs of Egypt . . . in which Cleopatra first

saw the approach of Julius Caesar and Marc Antony . . . and
. . . and so on and so on. Now, eh you ah . . . you'd better close
your eyes, my child, for a moment . . . in order to be better in
tune with the infinite . . .
(DOROTHY *closes her eyes and he rummages through her basket.*)
. . . we . . . we can't do these things without reaching out into
the infinite . . .
(*He flips out a photograph from the basket.*)

INSERT—A PHOTOGRAPH IN THE PROFESSOR'S HAND

*This is the picture of the farm, with DOROTHY and AUNT EM at
the gate, which we saw earlier on DOROTHY's table.*

BACK TO SCENE

*The PROFESSOR, evidently having gotten the cue he is looking for,
puts the photograph under his leg and brings his patter to a quick
close and gets down to business.*

PROFESSOR MARVEL (*cont'd*)   Yes, that's . . . that's all right. Now
you can open them. We'll gaze into the crystal!
(*gazing into it*)
Ah, what's this I see? A house . . . with a picket fence and a barn
with a weather vane and . . . of a . . . of a . . . running horse.

DOROTHY   That's our farm!

PROFESSOR MARVEL (*laughs*)   Yes . . . yes . . . there's . . . there's
. . . a woman . . . she's . . . she's wearing a . . . a . . .
polka-dot dress . . . her face is care-worn . . .

DOROTHY   That's Aunt Em!

PROFESSOR MARVEL (*as if reminded*)   Yes, her . . . her name is
Emily.

DOROTHY (*eagerly*)   That's right. What's she doing?

PROFESSOR MARVEL   Well . . . I . . . I can't quite see . . .
Why—she's crying!

DOROTHY   Oh!

PROFESSOR MARVEL   Someone has hurt her . . . someone has just about broken her heart . . .

DOROTHY *(in a small, guilty voice)*   Me?

PROFESSOR MARVEL   Well, it's . . . it's someone she loves very much. Someone she's been very kind to. Someone she's taken care of in sickness.

DOROTHY *(beginning to be affected)*   I had the measles once . . . and she stayed right by me every minute!

PROFESSOR MARVEL   Uh-huh.

DOROTHY   What's she doing now?*

PROFESSOR MARVEL *(dramatically)*   Eh, she's . . . *(gazing into the crystal)* . . . what's this? Why, she's . . . she's putting her hand on her heart! (DOROTHY *gasps*) Why, she's . . . she's dropping down on the bed!

DOROTHY *(distractedly)*   Oh, no! No!

PROFESSOR MARVEL   Eh, that's all. The crystal's gone dark.

DOROTHY *(rising)*   Oh, you . . . you don't suppose she could really be sick, do you? Oh!

PROFESSOR MARVEL   Oh, well, I . . .

DOROTHY   Oh, I've got to go home right away!

PROFESSOR MARVEL   But what's this? I thought you were going along with me!

DOROTHY *(picking up her basket)*   Oh, no! No, I have to get to her right away! Come on, Toto! Come on!

PROFESSOR MARVEL *(rising with photo in hand)*   Huh?

* At this point in the screenplay, John Lee Mahin introduced another foreshadowing of events in Oz that was eventually left out of the picture:

PROFESSOR MARVEL   She is going into a little bedroom . . .

DOROTHY   Has—has it poppies on the wallpaper?

PROFESSOR MARVEL   I said, "Poppies on the wallpaper."

LONG SHOT—REAR OF WAGON

DOROTHY *(as she comes scrambling down the steps) (picking up suitcase and* TOTO) Come on! Good-bye, Professor Marvel, and thanks a lot!
(She drops TOTO, *and they run out of scene.)*

LONG SHOT—PROFESSOR MARVEL

A gust of wind strikes the wagon and tosses the trees about, bringing down twigs and leaves. He glances up, concerned, and goes to his horse.

PROFESSOR MARVEL *(to his horse)* Better get under cover, Sylvester! There's a storm blowin' up—a whopper, to speak in the vernacular of the peasantry.
(worried, as he gazes after DOROTHY)
Poor little kid! I hope she gets home all right.

LAP DISSOLVE TO:
LONG SHOT—GALE FARM

By now the sky is dark and ominous. The wind is whistling. A cyclone is approaching.

LONG SHOT—BARNYARD

Chickens are running. The wind is blowing weeds and dust.

UNCLE HENRY *(running in with* HUNK) Hunk, get them horses loose! Where's Hickory? Hickory! Hickory! Doggone it! Hick—*

ZEKE comes running in from outside.

---

* Here a short scene of Hickory and his wind machine was filmed but cut from the final movie:

HICKORY   Right here.

CAMERA TRUCKS back to Hickory working on his wind machine.

UNCLE HENRY   Hey, what are you doing there?

HICKORY   This is my chance! The cyclone is coming. Let me show you what my machine can do! You see, it goes—

UNCLE HENRY   Doggone you! Help Hunk get them horses loose!

HICKORY *(exiting)*   All right—you'll be sorry.

UNCLE HENRY   Go on, hurry up! Hurry up, I tell you!

ZEKE *(terrified, looking up and out at the sky, pointing)* It's a twister . . . it's a twister!

The wind grows stronger. The horses run loose from the barn.

LONG SHOT—FARM

The CYCLONE is approaching.

EXTERIOR—BY KITCHEN DOOR

AUNT EM *(wildly)* Dorothy! Dorothy!

LONG SHOT—ROADWAY

DOROTHY and TOTO struggle against the wind. The cyclone is behind them.

LONG SHOT—BARNYARD

UNCLE HENRY and the farm hands turn a horse loose, and they run after it.

UNCLE HENRY   Come on! Everybody in the storm cellar!

ROADWAY—ANOTHER SHOT OF DOROTHY AND TOTO

Weeds and branches are blowing by them. She picks up TOTO.

LONG SHOT—STORM CELLAR

Everyone rushing to the storm cellar.

AUNT EM   Henry! Henry! I can't find Dorothy! She's somewhere out in the storm! Dorothy!

UNCLE HENRY   Gosh, we can't look for her now!

AUNT EM   Dorothy!

UNCLE HENRY   Come on! Get in the cellar! Hurry up!

They start to go down into the cellar.

LONG SHOT—GALE FARM

DOROTHY reaches the gate. CAMERA PANS as she comes to the house. When she opens the screen door, it flies off in the wind. She goes inside.

LONG SHOT—STORM CELLAR

ZEKE and HUNK are now exiting down into the cellar and pulling the door shut after them.

INT. FARMHOUSE

DOROTHY, carrying TOTO, hurries from room to room.

During all of this the SOUND of the wind has been increasing until it is almost unbearable.

DOROTHY *(wildly)*   Auntie Em! Auntie Em! Auntie Em!

LONG SHOT—STORM CELLAR

DOROTHY runs to the cellar door and tries to open it, but it will not budge. She then stamps on it with her foot.

DOROTHY   Auntie Em! Uncle Henry!
(She rushes back into the house.)

INT. DOROTHY'S BEDROOM

DOROTHY looks out of the window and turns back.

DOROTHY *(almost lost in the uproar)*   Auntie Em! Oh!

As the blast hits the house, the window blows in and strikes her on the back of the head. She falls over onto her bed.

MONTAGE—CLOSEUP—PRISM SHOT OF DOROTHY

Superimposed over shots of the whirling cyclone and the house whirling through space. These effects suggest the sensations of a person going under gas or ether.

This is the first scene of DOROTHY's delirium. Up to now, nothing is shown that hasn't actually happened in real life. This, therefore, is the first scene of the fantasy.

MEDIUM SHOT—BEDROOM

DOROTHY is beginning to pull herself up from the bed. She peers fearfully out of the window and sees the wreckage floating past: a chicken roost, a fence, a house, a buggy, a tree, a henhouse with a crowing rooster.

An OLD LADY in a rocking chair sails past. She is knitting busily and rocking, seemingly unaware that she is no longer on her front porch. The old lady waves as she floats out of sight, and a COW sails past that moos at DOROTHY mournfully. TOTO barks.

A CRATE OF FOWL goes gently past. A SMALL ROWBOAT goes by, TWO MEN rowing furiously at the oars. They tip their hats and drift out of sight.

MEDIUM SHOT—DOROTHY

She peers down at the swirling funnel of the cyclone.

DOROTHY *(shouting)*   We must be up inside the cyclone!

CLOSE SHOT—TOTO

peering out from under the bed.

MEDIUM SHOT—BEDROOM

DOROTHY sees MISS GULCH pedaling away grimly on her bicycle.

DOROTHY   Oh, Miss Gulch!

When MISS GULCH comes close to the CAMERA, her clothes change into a flying robe and pointed hat of a witch, and her bicycle fades into a broom. She gives a wild, weird peal of laughter.

LONG SHOT—CYCLONE

The house spins up in the swirling funnel of the cyclone and then parts company with it.

LONG SHOT—DOROTHY

Screaming as the bed spins and rolls around the floor.

LONG SHOT—PROCESS

The house begins to fall.

The house comes spiraling down through the air toward CAMERA, WHICH IS TILTED UP TOWARD IT. Eventually it hits CAMERA and blocks out the SCREEN.

MEDIUM SHOT—DOROTHY AND TOTO

as the house comes to a crashing halt.

DOROTHY   Oh!

There is dead silence on the SOUNDTRACK as DOROTHY gets off the bed with TOTO in her arms and picks up her basket and tiptoes to the door.

WIPE TO:
MEDIUM SHOT—FRONT DOOR—INTERIOR

As DOROTHY opens the door slowly and peers out, a blaze of color greets her. THIS IS THE FIRST TIME WE SEE TECHNICOLOR. The Kansas scenes were all sepia washes. The inside of the door is monochrome, to give more contrast. When the door is open, the country is shown—a picture of bright greens and blues.

As DOROTHY goes through the door, the CAMERA TRUCKS after her and then, over her shoulder, to a FULL SHOT of the MUNCHKIN COUNTRY. It is composed of sweeping hills and valleys and dips and waves in the ground; the grass is spangled with daisies; flowers grow everywhere, three or four times life-size, so that hollyhocks stand several feet in the air. The sky is bright blue with little white clouds; and a little stream runs near with huge lily pads on it.

Feeding the stream is an exquisite fountain. Surrounding the fountain are three or four steps, and to the back of it is Munchkinland's CIVIC CENTER, a quaint little piece of architecture. This is all close to the house in which Dorothy fell from Kansas.

The scene is quite empty of all signs of life, except the twittering of a bird or two in the distance.

LONG SHOT—DOROTHY

with TOTO in her arms. We get the faintly underscored strains of "Ding Dong! The Witch Is Dead!" The girl is looking around with an expression of delighted amazement.

DOROTHY   Toto, I've a feeling we're not in Kansas anymore . . .

To the strains of "Over the Rainbow," DOROTHY walks with TOTO in her arms. Some MUNCHKIN heads peer up above the bushes and then vanish again.

We must be over the rainbow!

LONG SHOT—THE COUNTRYSIDE

Suddenly a large, pink-tinted crystal BUBBLE, gleaming like a soap bubble, approaches, getting bigger and bigger. DOROTHY steps aside as it bounces gently in the air before her for a moment and then fades when it lands. The WITCH OF THE NORTH DISSOLVES IN.

CLOSEUP—DOROTHY

At the sight of the WITCH, she is astounded.

DOROTHY *(cont'd.) (to* TOTO*)*   Now I—I *know* we're not in Kansas.

LONGER ON SCENE

GLINDA comes gracefully forward. She chatters very brightly and quickly and puts in a high trill of a giggle wherever she can find room for it.

GLINDA   Are you a good witch—or a bad witch?

DOROTHY is so sure GLINDA can't be addressing her that she looks around behind her. But there is nobody there.

DOROTHY *(turning back)*   Who, me? Why—I'm not a witch at all. I'm Dorothy Gale from Kansas.

GLINDA *(pointing to* TOTO*)*   Oh, well, is *that* the witch?

CLOSE ON TOTO

GROUP SHOT—DOROTHY, WITCH, TOTO

DOROTHY   Who, Toto? Toto's my dog!

GLINDA *(puzzled)*   Well, I'm a little muddled—the Munchkins called me because a new witch has just dropped a house on the Wicked Witch of the East—and there's the house—and here *you* are—and that's all that's left of the Wicked Witch of the East.

GLINDA points, and we CUT IN A QUICK CLOSEUP of two RUBY SLIPPERS sticking out from under the house.

DOROTHY   Oh!

GLINDA   And so, what the Munchkins want to know is: Are you a good witch or a bad witch?

DOROTHY   Oh, but I've already told you, I'm not a witch at all— witches are old and ugly.
(There is a musical peal of laughter from behind the bushes and flowers. DOROTHY *starts and looks about.)*
What was that?

GLINDA *(smiling)*   The Munchkins. They're laughing because I *am* a witch. I'm Glinda, the Witch of the North.

DOROTHY   You *are*? *(curtsies)* Oh, I beg your pardon! But I've never heard of a beautiful witch before!

GLINDA   Only bad witches are ugly. The Munchkins are happy because you have freed them from the Wicked Witch of the East.

DOROTHY *(puzzled)*   Oh, but if you please, what are Munchkins?

The musical laughter comes again from the MUNCHKINS.

GLINDA   The little people who live in this land—it's Munchkinland . . . and you are their national heroine, my dear.
(GLINDA calls to the MUNCHKINS.)
It's all right—you may all come out and thank her!
(singing)
Come out, come out wherever you are.
And meet the young lady who fell from a star.

One by one the MUNCHKINS get up courage to tiptoe out to music.

GLINDA *(cont'd.) (singing)*
  She fell from the sky, she fell very far.
  And KANSAS she says is the name of the star.

MUNCHKINS *(singing)*
  KANSAS she says is the name of the star.

  By now the MUNCHKINS *are around* DOROTHY. *They are quaint, jolly-looking little men and women.*

GLINDA *(singing)*
  She brings you good news. Or haven't you heard?
  When she fell out of Kansas, a miracle occurred.

DOROTHY   It really was no miracle. What happened was just this:
(singing; modestly explaining to the MUNCHKINS*)*
The wind began to switch,
The house to pitch,
And suddenly the hinges started to unhitch.
Just then the witch
To satisfy an itch
Went flying on her broomstick thumbing for a hitch.

MUNCHKIN *(a braggart)*
  And OH what happened then was rich.

SEVERAL MUNCHKINS
  The house began to pitch,
  The kitchen took a slitch.

ALL OF THE MUNCHKINS
  It landed on the Wicked Witch in the middle of a ditch
  Which
  Was not a healthy sitch-
  Uation for
  The Wicked Witch.
  (dancing)
  The house began to pitch,
  The kitchen took a slitch.
  It landed on the Wicked Witch in the middle of a ditch
  Which

Was not a healthy sitch-
Uation for
The Wicked Witch
Who
Began to twitch
And was reduced
To just a stitch
Of what was once the Wicked Witch. (cheering)

A carriage drawn by ponies has driven up, and DOROTHY steps in.

MUNCHKIN NO. 1
We thank you very sweetly
For doing it so neatly.

MUNCHKIN NO. 2
You've killed her so completely
That we thank you very sweetly.
(handing her a bouquet)

GLINDA
Let the joyous news be spread
The Wicked Old Witch at last is dead!

CAMERA BOOMS as carriage moves forward, followed by a pro-
cession of MUNCHKIN SOLDIERS.

ALL MUNCHKINS *(with great gusto)*
Ding Dong, the witch is dead
Which old witch?
The wicked witch
Ding Dong, the wicked witch is dead!
Wake up, you sleepy head,
Rub your eyes,
Get out of bed.
Wake up, the wicked witch is dead!
She's gone where the goblins go
Below, below, below,
Yo ho let's open up and sing,
And ring the bells out:
Ding Dong! the merry-o

Sing it high,
Sing it low,
Let them know
The wicked witch is dead!

The carriage has stopped at the steps of Munchkinland's CIVIC
CENTER. FANFARE . . . and three HERALDS. Enter MAYOR,
who helps DOROTHY out of the carriage and takes her up the steps
to six CITY FATHERS, BARRISTER, etc.

MAYOR *(singing)*
As Mayor of the Munchkin City
In the County of the Land of Oz,
I welcome you most regally.

BARRISTER *(singing)*
But we've got to verify it legally.
To see . . .

MAYOR
To see . . .

BARRISTER
If she . . .

MAYOR
If she . . .

BARRISTER
Is morally, ethic'ly

CITY FATHER NO. 1
Spiritually, physically

CITY FATHER NO. 2
Positively, absolutely

ALL THE CITY FATHERS
Undeniably and reliably
DEAD!

GLINDA smiles.

CORONER (*walking up steps with a huge death certificate and sing-ing*)
As Coroner, I must aver,
I thoroughly examined her,
And she's not only MERELY dead,
She's really most SINCERELY dead.

MAYOR
Then this is a day of independence
For all the Munchkins and their descendants—

BARRISTER (*pompously*)
If any!

MAYOR
Yes, let the joyous news be spread
The Wicked Old Witch at last is dead!

They all cheer and dance. CAMERA PANS during the next lines showing the MUNCHKINS happily spreading the glad news.

ALL MUNCHKINS (*singing*)
Ding Dong, the witch is dead
Which old witch?
The wicked witch
Ding Dong, the wicked witch is dead!
Wake up, you sleepy head,
(SLEEPY HEADS *in a bird's nest wake up.*)
Rub your eyes,
Get out of bed.
Wake up, the wicked witch is dead!
She's gone where the goblins go
Below, below, below,
Yo ho let's open up and sing,
And ring the bells out:
Ding Dong! the merry-o
Sing it high,
Sing it low,
Let them know
The wicked witch is dead!

MUNCHKIN SOLDIERS parade and march.

LONG SHOT—CIVIC CENTER

DOROTHY is standing on the steps as THREE TINY TOTS dance through the line of SOLDIERS.

TINY TOTS *(singing as they dance on toe)*
We represent the Lullaby League, the Lullaby League, the
  Lullaby League,
And in the name of the Lullaby League,
We wish to welcome you to Munchkinland.

DOROTHY blows a kiss.

THREE TOUGH KIDS now clog-hop up to DOROTHY.

THREE TOUGH KIDS *(singing)*
We represent da Lollipop Guild, da Lollipop Guild, da Lollipop
  Guild
And in da name of da Lollipop Guild
We wish to welcome you to Munchkinland.

FULL SHOT—CIVIC CENTER

The THREE TOUGH KIDS hand DOROTHY a big lollipop.

OTHER MUNCHKINS, THE MAYOR, THE CITY FATHERS, etc. *(singing)*
We welcome you to Munchkinland
Tra-la-la-la-la-la
Tra-la-la, Tra-la-la
(little musical interlude)
Tra-la-la-la-la-la-la

MAYOR *(to DOROTHY)*
From now on you'll be history

BARRISTER
You'll be hist . . .

CITY FATHER
You'll be hist . . .

MAYOR

You'll be history.

GROUP

And we will glorify your name.

MAYOR

You will be a bust . . .

BARRISTER

Be a bust . . .

CITY FATHER

Be a bust . . .

GROUP

In the Hall of Fame!

ALL MUNCHKINS

Tra-la-la-la-la-la,
Tra-la-la, Tra-la-la
Tra-la-la-la-la-la-la—
Tra-la-la-la-la-la
Tra-la-la, Tra-la-la
Tra-la-la-la-la-la-la
Tra-la-la-la-la, Tra-la-la, Tra-la-la-la
Tra-la-la-la-la-la—

Suddenly on the last tra-la, the music stops with a terrific EXPLO-SION followed by a burst of RED SMOKE in front of DOROTHY's house.

The MUNCHKINS scatter and some fall flat on their faces with a wail of terror.

CLOSE SHOT—THE WICKED WITCH

The smoke clears away, leaving the WITCH OF THE WEST standing facing CAMERA.

CLOSEUP—DOROTHY

Terrified, she hugs TOTO close to her.

CLOSE SHOT—THE WICKED WITCH

She walks over to the farmhouse to look at the WICKED WITCH OF THE EAST.

MEDIUM SHOT—DOROTHY—GLINDA

DOROTHY *(in alarm and bewilderment)*   I thought you said she was dead!

GLINDA   That was her sister, the Wicked Witch of the East. This is the Wicked Witch of the West. And she's worse than the other one was.

MEDIUM SHOT—THE WICKED WITCH

She turns away from the farmhouse. CAMERA PANS as she turns to GLINDA and DOROTHY.

WITCH   Who killed my sister? Who killed the Witch of the East? *(to DOROTHY)* Was it *you*?

DOROTHY *(fearfully)*   No, No! It was an accident—I didn't mean to kill anybody!

WITCH   Well, my little pretty, I can cause accidents, too!

GLINDA *(quickly)*   Aren't you forgetting the ruby slippers?

WITCH   The slippers—yes, the slippers!
(She hurries to the house and is just about to snatch up the slippers when they vanish from under her hands and the feet shrivel up under the house.)
They're gone! The ruby slippers—what have you done with them? Give them back to me or I'll— *(turning back to GLINDA)*

GLINDA   It's too late!
(She points her wand at DOROTHY's feet.)
There they are, and there they'll stay!

CLOSEUP—DOROTHY'S FEET

in the RUBY SLIPPERS.

DOROTHY   Oh!

CLOSE SHOT—WITCH, GLINDA, DOROTHY

WITCH *(to both* GLINDA *and* DOROTHY, *in a frenzy)* Give me back my slippers! I'm the only one that knows how to use them—they're of no use to you!—Give them back to me—give them back!

GLINDA *(to* DOROTHY*)* Keep tight inside of them—their magic must be very powerful, or she wouldn't want them so badly!

WITCH *(furiously)* You stay out of this, Glinda, or I'll fix you as well!

GLINDA *(laughs)* Oh, ho-ho, rubbish! You have no power here! Be gone before somebody drops a house on you, too!

WITCH *(falling back as she looks up)* Very well—I'll bide my time—
(to DOROTHY*)*
—and as for you, my fine lady, it's true I can't attend to you here and now as I'd like; but just try to stay out of my way—just try! I'll get you, my pretty, and your little dog, too!

With a burst of laughter, she whirls around and vanishes in a burst of smoke and fire and a clap of thunder.

MEDIUM SHOT—GLINDA, DOROTHY

GLINDA *(to the* MUNCHKINS*)* It's all right—you can get up. She's gone. It's all right. You can all get up.

LONG SHOT—THE MUNCHKINS

rise to their feet and dust themselves off sheepishly.

CLOSE SHOT—GLINDA AND DOROTHY

GLINDA *(daintily)* Ooh, what a smell of sulfur!
(to DOROTHY*)*
I'm afraid you've made rather a bad enemy of the Wicked Witch of the West. The sooner you get out of Oz altogether, the safer you'll sleep, my dear.

DOROTHY Oh, I'd give anything to get out of Oz altogether; but which is the way back to Kansas? I can't go the way I came!

The MUNCHKINS all shake their heads regretfully.

L. Frank Baum, the author of *The Wonderful Wizard of Oz*.

The snowstorm in the Broadway musical extravaganza of *The Wizard of Oz*, 1903. Courtesy the Billy Rose Collection, the New York Public Library at Lincoln Center.

Mervyn LeRoy, the producer, and Victor Fleming, the director (holding Toto), with Judy Garland and the Singer Midgets. (© 1939 Loew's, Inc. Renewed 1966 MGM, Inc.)

Noel Langley.
COURTESY ALJEAN HARMETZ.

Florence Ryerson. COURTESY THE
BILLY ROSE COLLECTION, THE NEW
YORK PUBLIC LIBRARY AT LINCOLN
CENTER.

Edgar Allan Woolf. COURTESY THE
BILLY ROSE COLLECTION, THE NEW
YORK PUBLIC LIBRARY AT LINCOLN
CENTER.

John Lee Mahin. COURTESY
ALJEAN HARMETZ.

E. Y. Harburg and Harold Arlen. Courtesy Edward Jablonski and ASCAP.

King Vidor.

Judy Garland with Maud
Gage Baum, the author's
widow. (© 1939 Loew's,
Inc. Renewed 1966
MGM, Inc.)

The Cowardly Lion (Bert Lahr), the Tin Man (Jack Haley), Toto, Dorothy (Judy Garland), the Wizard (Frank Morgan), and the Scarecrow (Ray Bolger). (© 1939 Loew's, Inc. Renewed 1966 MGM, Inc.)

DOROTHY: Uncle Henry, Auntie Em! Don't let 'em take Toto!
(page 42) (© 1939 Loew's, Inc. Renewed 1966 MGM, Inc.)

GLINDA: *Come out, come out wherever you are.*
And meet the young lady who fell from a star. (page 54)
(© 1939 Loew's, Inc. Renewed 1966 MGM, Inc.)

SCARECROW: Did I scare you? (page 67) (© 1939 Loew's, Inc. Renewed 1966 MGM, Inc.)

SCARECROW: Oh, no! It's just that she doesn't like little green *worms*! (page 71) (© 1939 Loew's, Inc. Renewed 1966 MGM, Inc.)

TIN MAN: Bah! Let her try and make a beehive out of me! (page 76)
(© 1939 Loew's, Inc. Renewed 1966 MGM, Inc.)

LION: Hah, put 'em up, put 'em up! (page 78) (© 1939 Loew's, Inc.
Renewed 1966 MGM, Inc.)

DOROTHY: Look—Emerald City is closer and prettier than ever! (page 86) (© 1939 Loew's, Inc. Renewed 1966 MGM, Inc.)

CABBY AND CITIZENS: *That's how we laugh the day away In the Merry Old Land of Oz* . . . (page 90) (© 1939 Loew's, Inc. Renewed 1966 MGM, Inc.)

WITCH: It's so kind of you to visit me in my loneliness. (page 106)
(© 1939 Loew's, Inc. Renewed 1966 MGM, Inc.)

LION: Oh, look! Look! Oh, look . . . ! (page 103) (© 1939 Loew's, Inc. Renewed 1966 MGM, Inc.)

WITCH: I'm melting! Melting! (page 119) (© 1939 Loew's, Inc. Renewed 1966 MGM, Inc.)

WIZARD: I, your Wizard *par ardua ad alta*, am about to embark upon a hazardous and technically unexplainable journey into the outer stratosphere . . . (page 125) (© 1939 Loew's, Inc. Renewed 1966 MGM, Inc.)

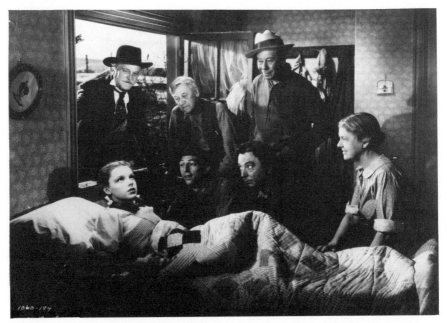

DOROTHY: Doesn't anybody believe me? (page 131) (© 1939 Loew's, Inc. Renewed 1966 MGM, Inc.)

Ray Bolger does a series of splits in "The Scarecrow's Dance."
(page 134) (© 1939 Loew's, Inc. Renewed 1966 MGM, Inc.)

Jack Haley is turned into "The Beehive." (page 136) (© 1939 Loew's, Inc. Renewed 1966 MGM, Inc.)

The trees of the Haunted Forest shiver as Judy Garland and the others sing "The Jitterbug." (page 138) (© 1939 Loew's, Inc. Renewed 1966 MGM, Inc.)

Ray Bolger carries the Witch's broomstick in "The Triumphant Procession." (page 142) (© 1939 Loew's, Inc. Renewed 1966 MGM, Inc.)

GLINDA   No, that's true. The only person who might know would be the great and wonderful Wizard of Oz himself.

All the MUNCHKINS bow deeply at the name.

DOROTHY *(noticing the* MUNCHKINS' *reaction)*   The Wizard of Oz? Is he good or is he wicked?

GLINDA   Oh, very good; but very mysterious. He lives in the Emerald City, and that's a long journey from here. Did you bring your broomstick with you?

DOROTHY   No, I'm afraid I didn't.

GLINDA   Well, then, you'll have to walk. The Munchkins will see you safely to the border of Munchkinland. And remember, never let those ruby slippers off your feet for a moment, or you will be at the mercy of the Wicked Witch of the West. *(kisses her on forehead)*

DOROTHY   But how do I start for Emerald City?

GLINDA   It's always best to start at the beginning. And all you do is follow the Yellow Brick Road. *(pointing with wand)*

PAN SHOT—

as DOROTHY walks forward.

DOROTHY   But what happens if I—

MEDIUM SHOT—THE COUNTRYSIDE FROM DOROTHY'S VIEWPOINT

GLINDA   Just follow the Yellow Brick Road.

She steps back, and the large pink-tinted crystal BUBBLE reappears. The bubble slowly rises, carrying GLINDA away, as the MUNCHKINS rush toward it.

MUNCHKINS   Good-bye! Good-bye! Good-bye! *(etc.)*

MEDIUM SHOT—DOROTHY

DOROTHY   My! People come and go so quickly here!

The MUNCHKINS laugh.

*CAMERA PANS down to DOROTHY'S RUBY SLIPPERS as she
steps onto the Yellow Brick Road.*

DOROTHY   Follow the Yellow Brick Road. Follow the Yellow Brick
Road?

MAYOR   Follow the Yellow Brick Road.

MUNCHKIN MAN   Follow the Yellow Brick Road.

MUNCHKIN WOMAN   Follow the Yellow Brick Road.

BARRISTER   Follow the Yellow Brick Road.

ALL MUNCHKINS *(singing)*
Follow the yellow brick road
Follow the yellow brick road,
Follow, follow, follow, follow,
Follow the yellow brick road.
Follow the yellow brick,
Follow the yellow brick,
Follow the yellow brick road.

*FIVE LITTLE FIDDLERS dance out behind DOROTHY and
lead the procession of MUNCHKINS behind her and TOTO.*

You're off to see the Wizard,
The Wonderful Wizard of Oz.
You'll find he is a Whiz of a Wiz,
If ever a Wiz there was.
If ever, oh ever a Wiz there was,
The Wizard of Oz
Is one becoz
Becoz, becoz, becoz, becoz, becoz
Becoz of the wonderful things he does.
You're off to see the Wizard,
The Wonderful Wizard of Oz.

*The quaint little procession marches off as DOROTHY skips down
the Yellow Brick Road. The FIVE FIDDLERS play all the way
until they reach the boundary of Munchkinland.*

LONG SHOT—BOUNDARY

with Yellow Brick Road in foreground and hills and fields in background. As the MUNCHKINS finish their song, they wave and call cheery good-byes. DOROTHY turns and waves good-bye and continues on her way.

LAP DISSOLVE TO:
TRUCK SHOT—DOROTHY

She is walking along the Yellow Brick Road. TOTO is trotting beside her. She stops as the Yellow Brick Road crosses another one. She looks up and down, puzzled.

DOROTHY Follow the Yellow Brick Road, follow the Yellow—Now which way do we go?

VOICE Pardon me. That way is a very nice way.

LONG SHOT—SCARECROW

He is hanging awkwardly on the pole, with his arm pointing to the right down the road. His painted face strangely resembles our old friend HUNK's.

DOROTHY Who said that?

CLOSEUP—DOROTHY

She looks around for the voice. TOTO barks at the SCARECROW.

DOROTHY Don't be silly, Toto. Scarecrows don't talk.

SCARECROW *(pointing to the left)* It's pleasant down that way, too.

DOROTHY *(to* TOTO*)* That's funny. Wasn't he pointing the other way?

SCARECROW *(now pointing in both directions)* Of course, people do go both ways!

DOROTHY Why, you *did* say something, didn't you?

The SCARECROW shakes his head, then stops and nods it instead.

DOROTHY   Are you doing that on purpose—or can't you make up your mind?

SCARECROW   That's the trouble. I can't make up my mind. I haven't got a brain—only straw. *(showing her)*

DOROTHY   How can you talk if you haven't got a brain?

SCARECROW   I don't know. But some people without brains do an awful lot of talking, don't they?

DOROTHY *(speculatively)*   Yes—I guess you're right.
(impressed by such a truth)
Well, we haven't really met properly, have we?

SCARECROW   Why, no.

DOROTHY *(curtsying)*   How do you do?

SCARECROW *(nodding politely)*   How do you do?

DOROTHY   Very well, thank you.

SCARECROW   Oh, I'm not feeling at all well. You see, it's very tedious being stuck up here all day long with a pole up your back.

DOROTHY   Oh, dear! That must be terribly uncomfortable. Can't you get down?

SCARECROW   Down? *(trying to reach in back of him)* No. You see, I'm—well, I'm—

DOROTHY *(to his assistance)*   Oh, well, here—let me help you!

SCARECROW   Oh, that's very kind of you—very kind.

DOROTHY *(puzzled—as she works)*   Well, oh, dear—I don't quite see how I can—

SCARECROW   Of course, I'm not bright about doing things, but if you'll just bend the nail down in the back, maybe I'll slip off and come—

DOROTHY *(bending down the nail)*   Oh yes!

SCARECROW *(as he slips off to the ground)*   Ohhhh!

(As he lands, his coat bursts open, and straw falls out from his abdomen.)
Whoops! *(laughs)* There goes some of me again!

DOROTHY *(horrified)*   Oh! Does it hurt you?

SCARECROW *(blithely)*   Oh, no. I just keep picking it up and putting it back in again.
(He stuffs the straw back into his coat. He gets up and stretches himself luxuriously.)

DOROTHY   Oh!

SCARECROW   My! It's good to be free!
(He whirls around and promptly falls over a broken fence rail.)

DOROTHY   Oh! *(screams)* Ohhh! Oh!

SCARECROW *(sitting up with a hopeful smile)*   Did I scare you?

DOROTHY   No, no. I—I just thought you hurt yourself.

SCARECROW   But I didn't scare you . . . ?

DOROTHY *(as practical as Kansas)*   No, of course not.

SCARECROW *(dolefully)*   I didn't think so.
(A CROW *lights on his shoulder at this moment.)*
Boo! Scat! Boo!
(The CROW *picks a piece of straw and flies off with it.)*
(to DOROTHY*)*
You see, I can't even scare a crow! They come for miles around just to eat in my field and . . . and laugh in my face.
(almost weeps)
Oh, I'm a *failure,* because I haven't got a brain!

DOROTHY   Well, what would you do with a brain if you had one?

SCARECROW   Do? Why, if I had a brain I could—
(goes into his song and amusing dance)
I could while away the hours
Conferrin' with the flowers
Consultin' with the rain
And my head, I'd be scratchin'

While my thoughts were busy hatchin'
If I only had a brain.

DOROTHY helps him up.

I'd unravel ev'ry riddle
For any individ'le
In trouble or in pain

DOROTHY *(singing)*
With the thoughts you'd be thinkin'
You could be another Lincoln,
If you only had a brain.

SCARECROW *(singing)*
Oh, I could tell you why
The ocean's near the shore,
I could think of things I never thunk before
And then I'd sit and think some more.

I would not be just a nuffin'
My head all full of stuffin'
My heart all full of pain.
I would dance and be merry
Life would be a ding-a-derry
If I only had a brain—Whoa!

At the finish, he falls to the road. DOROTHY picks up some of his
straw and rushes over to him to stuff it back in again.

DOROTHY Wonderful! *(shaking his hand)* Why, if our scarecrow
back in Kansas could do that, the crows'd be scared to pieces!

SCARECROW They would?

DOROTHY Hmm.

SCARECROW Where's Kansas?

DOROTHY That's where I live. And I want to get back there so
badly, I'm going all the way to Emerald City to get the Wizard of
Oz to help me.

* See Appendix A: The Scarecrow's Dance, pp. 134–135.

SCARECROW   You're going to see a Wizard?

DOROTHY   Um-hmmm.

SCARECROW *(with a sudden idea)*   Do you think if I went with you, this Wizard would give me some brains?

DOROTHY   I couldn't say. *(then practically)* But even if he didn't, you'd be no worse off than you are now.

SCARECROW   Yes, that's true.

DOROTHY   But maybe you better not. I've got a witch mad at me, and you might get into trouble.

SCARECROW   Witch? Hmm! I'm not afraid of a witch. I'm not afraid of anything—
(in a whisper with a look around)—oh, except a lighted match. *(touches his straw)*

DOROTHY *(in a low voice)*   I don't blame you for that.

SCARECROW *(tensely)*   But I'd face a whole box full of them for the chance of getting some brains. *(pleading)* Look, I won't be any trouble, because I don't eat a thing; and I won't try to manage things, because I can't think. Uh . . . won't you take me with you?

DOROTHY *(warmly)*   Why, of *course,* I will!

SCARECROW *(leaping into the air)*   Hooray! We're off to see a Wizard!
(sinking down on her)

DOROTHY *(holding him up with difficulty)*   Oh, well, you're not starting out very well.

SCARECROW   Oh, I'll try—really I will.

DOROTHY   To Oz!

SCARECROW   To Oz!

They link arms and go into Marching Song.

DOROTHY and SCARECROW *(singing)*

We're off to see the Wizard,
The Wonderful Wizard of Oz.
We hear he is a Whiz of a Wiz
If ever a Wiz there was.
If ever, oh ever a Wiz there was,
The Wizard of Oz
Is one becoz
Becoz, becoz, becoz, becoz, becoz
Becoz of the wonderful things he does.
We're off to see the Wizard,
The Wonderful Wizard of Oz.

LAP DISSOLVE TO:
LONG SHOT—THE YELLOW BRICK ROAD

Running between fields and orchards. Along the road come DORO-
THY and the SCARECROW. They halt beside some old, gnarled
apple trees with twisted branches laden with large red apples. CAM-
ERA TRUCKS to show that the WITCH is in the shadows behind
one of the trees. She slinks away.

DOROTHY   Oh, apples! Oh . . . look! Oh! Oh!

MEDIUM SHOT—DOROTHY AND TREES

She picks an apple. At once the end of the branch seizes the apple in
a clawlike grab and takes it back, and the other slaps DOROTHY's
hand.

DOROTHY   Ouch!

FIRST TREE   What do you think you're doing?

DOROTHY   We've been walking a long ways, and I was hungry
and—*(suddenly, she blinks)* Did you say something?

FIRST TREE *(to* SECOND TREE*)*   She was hungry!

SECOND TREE   She was hungry!

FIRST TREE *(back to* DOROTHY*)*   Well, how would you like to have
someone come along and pick something off of you?

DOROTHY *(woefully)*   Oh, dear! I keep forgetting I'm not in Kansas.

SCARECROW   Come along, Dorothy, you don't want any of *those* apples. Hmmm!

FIRST TREE   Are you hinting my apples aren't what they ought to be?

SCARECROW   Oh, no! It's just that she doesn't like little green *worms*!

FIRST TREE   Oh, you! *(grabbing* DOROTHY, *who screams)*

The SCARECROW fights the tree as she struggles free.

SECOND TREE   You can't do that to me!

SCARECROW *(to* DOROTHY*)*   I'll show you how to get apples.

He puts his thumbs in his ears and waggles his fingers at them.

FIRST TREE takes an apple, swings its branch like a pitcher, and throws an apple at the SCARECROW and knocks him down. The SECOND TREE follows suit.

DOROTHY   Oh! Oh!

LONG SHOT—SCARECROW

running away from the trees, with apples pelting after him. DOROTHY runs after him out of the way.

SCARECROW   Aha! Hooray *(he begins picking them up)* I guess that did it! Help yourself!

MEDIUM SHOT—DOROTHY (THE TIN MAN'S LITTLE COTTAGE IN BACKGROUND)—PAN SHOT

She runs to gather up the apples and falls on her hands and knees to pick one up. CAMERA is now in:

CLOSE SHOT—

As DOROTHY's hand closes in on the apple, she sees a tin foot just beside it. She raps on it and then looks up, and the CAMERA PANS SLOWLY up the figure of the TIN MAN. His face, strangely enough, looks just like Hickory's.

MEDIUM SHOT—DOROTHY, TIN MAN

She scrambles to her feet, examining him.

DOROTHY *(raps on him)*   Why, it's a man! A man made out of tin!

SCARECROW   What?

DOROTHY   Yes! Oh, look! *(she raps on his chest)*

A creaky, rusty sound comes from the TIN MAN.

TIN MAN *(almost inaudibly)*   Oil can! Oil can!

DOROTHY *(to TIN MAN)*   Did you say something?

TIN MAN *(still in a hoarse creak)*   Oil can!

DOROTHY   He said oil can!

SCARECROW   Oil can what?

DOROTHY   Oil can? Oh! Oh!

TIN MAN   Ahh . . .

DOROTHY *(finding oil can)*   Here it is! Where do you want to be oiled first?

TIN MAN   My mouth . . . my mouth!

SCARECROW   He said his mouth!
(He oils the TIN MAN's mouth and hands the oil can to DOROTHY.)
The other side!

DOROTHY   Yes . . .

DOROTHY sends a drop or two by the TIN MAN's mouth.

TIN MAN *(clearing his throat, as his joints squeak)*   M—m—my, my, my, my, my, my, my goodness! I can talk again! Oh, oil my arms, please! Oil my elbows! Oh! Oh!

DOROTHY *(as she takes the can from SCARECROW and starts working on his arm joints)*   Here.

TIN MAN   Oh! Oh!

The SCARECROW oils the other arm.

DOROTHY *(lowering his ax)*   Oh.

TIN MAN   Oh!

DOROTHY   Did that hurt?

TIN MAN   No, it feels wonderful! I've held that ax up for ages. Oh!

DOROTHY   Goodness! How did you ever get like this?

TIN MAN   Oh, well, 'bout a year ago, I was chopping that tree, when suddenly it began to rain.

DOROTHY   Oh!

TIN MAN   And right in the middle of a chop, I—I rusted solid. I've been that way ever since. Oh.

As he talks, the SCARECROW and DOROTHY are working his joints.

DOROTHY   Well, you're perfect now.

TIN MAN *(to SCARECROW)*   My—my neck! My—my neck! *(back to DOROTHY)* Perfect? Oh, bang on my chest if you think I'm perfect. Go ahead—bang on it!

DOROTHY raps on his chest, which echoes.

SCARECROW   Beautiful! What an echo!

TIN MAN   It's empty.
(He looks around, then lowers his voice as though telling a terrible secret.)
The tinsmith forgot to give me a heart.

DOROTHY and SCARECROW   No heart?

TIN MAN   No heart!

DOROTHY   Oh.

TIN MAN   All hollow!
(He bangs on his chest and knocks himself against a tree stump. They go to help him, but he holds them off.)

(singing)
When a man's an empty kettle
He should be on his mettle
And yet I'm torn apart
Just because I'm presumin'
That I could be kind-a human
If I only had a heart.

I'd be tender, I'd be gentle
And awful sentimental
Regarding love and art
I'd be friends with the sparrows
And the boy who shoots the arrows,
If I only had a heart.
(standing)

Picture me . . . a balcony . . .
Above a voice sings low—

SNOW WHITE'S VOICE *(comes in singing)
Wherefore art thou, Romeo?

TIN MAN
(two beats) I hear a beat.
(two beats) How sweet!
Just to register emotion.
"Jealousy," "devotion"
And really feel the part
I could stay young and chipper
And I'd lock it with a zipper
If I only had a heart.

He goes into a dance. As the number finishes, DOROTHY and the
SCARECROW are having a whispered conversation. Just as he fin-
ishes, the TIN MAN's joints lock, and DOROTHY and the SCARE-
CROW come over to help. The TIN MAN staggers back with DOR-
OTHY and knocks the SCARECROW over.

---

* Although Yip Harburg was obviously referring to Shakespeare's Juliet, the studio hired
Adriana Caselotti (who had been the voice for Walt Disney's Snow White) to record this one
line in the Tin Man's song.

DOROTHY   Oh, oh . . .

TIN MAN   *(landing on tree stump)*   Oh!

DOROTHY   . . . oh, oh, oh, are you all right?

TIN MAN   I'm afraid I'm a little rusty yet. Oh.

DOROTHY   Oh, dear. That was wonderful! You know, we were just wondering why you couldn't come with us to the Emerald City to ask the Wizard of Oz for a heart!

TIN MAN   Well, suppose the Wizard wouldn't give me one when we got there?

DOROTHY   Oh, but he will! *(in distress)* He must! We've come such a long way already—

A wild peal of laughter.

CAMERA PANS up to roof of TIN MAN's cottage, and perched on the roof is the WICKED WITCH.

WITCH   You call that *long*? Why, you've just begun! Helping the little lady along, are you, my fine gentlemen? Well, stay away from her! *(savagely to the SCARECROW)* Or I'll stuff a mattress with you!

MEDIUM SHOT—THREE

The SCARECROW winces. The TIN MAN points to him and then to himself.

WITCH   And *you*! I'll use you for a beehive! Here, Scarecrow! Want to play ball?
(She throws down a ball of fire with a scream of laughter.)

LONG SHOT—THREE

The ball of fire drops down in front of the SCARECROW, and he leaps wildly in terror. Dorothy screams.

SCARECROW   Oh! Look out! Fire! I'm burning! I'm burning! Oh! Take it away!

The TIN MAN slams his tin hat down on the fireball to put it out.

LONG SHOT—WITCH

on roof laughs again and vanishes in a puff of red smoke.

CLOSEUP—DOROTHY

with TOTO in her arms, as smoke clears

MEDIUM SHOT—THREE

The SCARECROW gets up from the ground. The TIN MAN puts his hat on again.

SCARECROW *(angrily)* I'm not afraid of her! I'll see you get safely to the Wizard now. Whether I get a brain or not! Stuff a mattress with me! Heh!
(He snaps his fingers.)

TIN MAN *(heartily)* I'll see you reach the Wizard, whether I get a heart or not! Beehive! Bah! Let her try and make a beehive out of me!
(He snaps his fingers.) *

DOROTHY *(happily)* Oh, you're the best friends anybody ever had! And it's funny, but I feel as if I've known you all the time—but I couldn't have, could I?

SCARECROW I don't see how. You weren't around when I was stuffed and sewn together, were you?

TIN MAN And I was standing over there, rusting for the longest time.

DOROTHY *(still puzzled)* Still—I wish I could remember . . . but I guess it doesn't matter, anyway—we know each other now, don't we?

SCARECROW That's right.

TIN MAN We do!

They all laugh.

SCARECROW *(offering his arm to DOROTHY)* To Oz!

* See Appendix B: The Beehive, pp. 136–137.

TIN MAN *(offering his arm to her)* To Oz!

They march off, singing. TOTO runs out and joins them.

DOROTHY, TIN MAN, and SCARECROW
We're off to see the Wizard
The Wonderful Wizard of Oz.
We hear he is a Whiz of a Wiz
If ever a Wiz there was.
If ever, oh ever a Wiz there was,
The Wizard of Oz
Is one becoz
Becoz, becoz, becoz, becoz, becoz
Becoz of the wonderful things he does.
We're off to see the Wizard,
The Wonderful Wizard of Oz.

LAP DISSOLVE TO:
LONG SHOT—A DARK AND EERIE FOREST

The comrades are coming along the Yellow Brick Road.

They move forward slowly and stop.

DOROTHY Oh, I don't like this forest! It's—it's dark and creepy!

SCARECROW Of course, I don't know, but I think it'll get darker before it gets lighter.

DOROTHY Do—do you suppose we'll meet any wild animals?

TIN MAN Mmm—we might.

DOROTHY Oh—

SCARECROW Animals that—that eat straw?

TIN MAN *(nonchalantly)* Uh, some. But mostly lions and tigers and bears.

DOROTHY Lions?

SCARECROW And tigers?

TIN MAN *(nodding)* And bears.

DOROTHY   Oh! Lions and tigers and bears. Oh my!

LONG SHOT—THREE

They look around and slowly start to run.

ALL   *(reciting in rhythm to their steps, each time louder and faster)*   Lions and tigers and bears!

DOROTHY   Oh my!

ALL   Lions and tigers and bears!

DOROTHY   Oh my!

ALL   Lions and tigers and bears!

DOROTHY   Oh my!

ALL   Lions and tigers and bears!

DOROTHY   Oh my!

A roar from ahead of them.

SCARECROW *(pointing)*   Oh, look!

DOROTHY   Oh!

LONG SHOT—COWARDLY LION

in distance roars. He advances; they retreat. He advances; they retreat. He advances; they retreat. He leaps in the air and comes down on all fours, scattering the others. He straightens up in a boxer's stance and then waltzes menacingly, doing some very fancy shadowboxing.

LION *(growling)*   Hah, put 'em up, put 'em up! Which one of ya first? I'll fight ya both together if ya want. I'll fight ya with one paw tied behind my back. *(puts paw behind back)* I'll fight ya standin' on one foot! *(stands on one foot)* I'll fight ya with my eyes closed. *(closes his eyes, then opens them—to* TIN MAN*)* Ohhhh—pullin' an ax on me, eh? *(to* SCARECROW*)* Sneakin' up on me, eh? Why . . . *(growls)*

TIN MAN   Here, here. Go 'way and let us alone.

LION Oh, scared, huh? Afraid, huh? Ha! How long can ya stay fresh in that can? *(laughs)* Come on! Get up and fight, ya shiverin' junkyard. *(to* SCARECROW*)* Put ya hands up, ya lopsided bag of hay!

SCARECROW *(reproachfully)* Now, that's getting personal, Lion!

TIN MAN Yes, get up and teach him a lesson!

SCARECROW Well, what's wrong with you teachin' him?

TIN MAN Ah—well—well, I hardly know him.

CLOSE SHOT—TOTO

barking.

LION I'll get you anyway, peewee! *(growls)*

DOROTHY No!
*(*TOTO *jumps into the bushes with the* LION *growling after him.* DOROTHY *grabs* TOTO *in her arms. She slaps the* LION *smartly on the nose.)*
Shame on you!

LION *(bawling)* What did ya do that for? I didn't bite him!

DOROTHY No, but you *tried* to! It's bad enough picking on a straw man, but when you go around picking on poor little dogs—

LION *(sniffing pathetically)* Well, ya didn't have to go and hit me, did ya? Is my nose bleedin'? *(sobbing)*

DOROTHY *(severely)* Well, of course not! My goodness, what a fuss you're making! Well, naturally when you go around picking on things weaker than you are—why, you're nothing but a great big coward!

LION *(to* DOROTHY, *with great self-pity, playing with his tail)* You're right, I *am* a coward! I haven't any courage at all! I even scare myself. Look at the circles under my eyes! I haven't slept in weeks!

TIN MAN Why don't you try counting sheep?

LION That doesn't do any good—I'm afraid of 'em! *(bawling)*

SCARECROW   Oh, that's too bad. *(to* DOROTHY*)* Don't you think the Wizard could help him, too?

DOROTHY   I don't see why not. *(to* LION*)* Why don't you come along with us? We're on our way to see the Wizard now. *(pointing to the* TIN MAN*)* To get him a heart.

TIN MAN *(pointing to the* SCARECROW*)*   And him a brain.

DOROTHY   I'm sure he could give you some courage!

LION   Well, wouldn't you feel degraded to be seen in the company of a cowardly lion? *I* would. *(sobbing)*

DOROTHY   No, of course not!

LION *(still sniffling)*   Gee, that—that's awfully nice of ya. My life has been simply unbearable.

DOROTHY   Oh, well, it's all right now. The Wizard'll fix everything.

LION *(emotionally as they walk)*   It—It's been in me so long, I just gotta tell ya how I feel.

DOROTHY *(taking his arm)*   Well, come on!

LION *(singing)*
Yeah, it's sad, believe me, missy,
When you're born to be a sissy,
Without the vim and verve.
But I could show my prowess,
Be a lion not a mowess,
If I only had the nerve.

I'm afraid there's no denyin'
I'm just a dandelion,
A fate I don't deserve.
I'd be brave as a blizzard . . .

TIN MAN *(singing)*
I'd be gentle as a lizard . . .

SCARECROW *(singing)*
I'd be clever as a gizzard . . .

DOROTHY *(singing)*
  If the Wizard is a wizard who will serve.

SCARECROW *(singing)*
  Then I'm sure to get a brain . . .

TIN MAN *(singing)*
  . . . a heart

DOROTHY *(singing)*
  . . . a home

LION *(singing)*
  . . . the nerve!

ALL *(singing, arm in arm)*
  Oh, we're off to see the Wizard,
  The Wonderful Wizard of Oz.
  We hear he is a Whiz of a Wiz
  If ever a Wiz there was.
  If ever, oh ever a Wiz there was,
  The Wizard of Oz
  Is one becoz
  Becoz, becoz, becoz, becoz, becoz
  Becoz of the wonderful things he does.
  We're off to see the Wizard,
  The Wonderful Wizard of Oz.

MUSICAL FADE OUT

CLOSEUP—CRYSTAL
In it we see the four friends marching arm in arm. CAMERA PULLS BACK to show the WITCH OF THE WEST gazing into it and laughing. Near her sits her familiar winged chimpanzee, NIKKO, watching the crystal.

WITCH *(laughing)* Aha, so you won't take warning, eh? All the worse for you, then—I'll take care of you now instead of later! Hah!
(She turns, mixes poison, and returns to crystal.)
When I gain those ruby slippers, my power will be the greatest in Oz!

(holding poison over crystal)
And now, my beauties! . . . something with poison in it, I think;
with poison in it, but attractive to the eye and soothing to the
smell! Heh, heh, heh, heh, heh, heh!
*(The poppy field fades into the crystal as she runs her fingers over
it.)*
Poppies . . . poppies . . . poppies will put them to sleep . . .
sleep . . . now they'll sleep . . .

DISSOLVE TO:
LONG SHOT—POPPY FIELD

*CAMERA PANS over the field to the FOUR in the far distance,
marching.*

MEDIUM SHOT—FOUR

They suddenly halt.

DOROTHY *(pointing)* There's Emerald City!

LONG SHOT—EMERALD CITY

*shooting across the poppy field. In the far distance stands the glit-
tering towers and domes of the EMERALD CITY.*

DOROTHY *(cont'd.) (in rapture)* Oh, we're almost there at last! At
last!

CLOSE SHOT—FOUR

DOROTHY *(cont'd.)* It's beautiful, isn't it? Just like I knew it would
be! He really must be a wonderful Wizard to live in a city like that!

LION Well, come on, then. What are we waiting for?

SCARECROW Nothing! Let's hurry!

DOROTHY Yes, let's run!

LION Yeah!

*They all run into the poppy field. The SCARECROW and TIN
MAN quickly run on ahead as the COWARDLY LION and DORO-
THY lag behind.*

SCARECROW   Come on! Come on!

TIN MAN   Hurry! Hurry!

SCARECROW   Oh, look!

LONG SHOT—EMERALD CITY

with Yellow Brick Road beyond poppies.

LONG SHOT—POPPY FIELD

TIN MAN   Oh!

SCARECROW   Come on!

TIN MAN   Look! You can see it here! It's wonderful! Emerald City!

CAMERA PANS with DOROTHY as she struggles through the poppies. A puzzled look comes on her face.

DOROTHY *(panting)*   Oh . . . oh, what's happening? What is it? *(putting her hand to her forehead)*
I can't run anymore. . . . I'm so sleepy . . .

SCARECROW   Here, give us your hands and we'll pull you along.

DOROTHY   Oh, no, please—I have to rest for just a minute. Toto . . . where's Toto?

CLOSEUP—TOTO

fast asleep.

LONG SHOT—POPPY FIELD

DOROTHY sinks down and falls asleep.

SCARECROW   Oh, you can't rest now—We're nearly there.*

* Cut from the film here was another scene in the Witch's tower room:

WITCH *(laughing)*   Call away! Call away! She won't hear any of *you* again; and there's nothing you can do about it, either! *(laughs)*
(to NIKKO*)*
Bring me my wishing cap. I'll call the Winged Monkeys to fetch me those slippers! Hurry! Hurry! Hurry! Hurry!
*(*NIKKO *goes out of shot.)*
It worked very smoothly!

CLOSEUP—TIN MAN

begins to cry.

FULL SHOT—THREE

standing around DOROTHY.

SCARECROW *(to* TIN MAN*)* Don't cry—you'll rust yourself again!

LION *(slowly sinking down)* Comin' to think of it forty winks *(yawns)* wouldn't be bad . . . *(yawns)*

SCARECROW Don't you start it, too!

The SCARECROW and TIN MAN grab his arms and stand him up again.

TIN MAN No! We ought to try and carry Dorothy.

SCARECROW I don't think I could . . . but we could try.

TIN MAN Let's.

SCARECROW Yes.

They both let go of the LION so they can help DOROTHY. He falls behind them flat on his back, fast asleep.

TIN MAN *(seeing* LION*)* Oh, now look at him! This is terrible!

SCARECROW Here, Tin Man—help me.

TIN MAN Oh!

SCARECROW *(trying to lift* DOROTHY*)* Uh! Oh, this is terrible! Can't budge her an inch!
(looking to TIN MAN*)*
This is a spell, this is!

TIN MAN It's the Wicked Witch! What'll we do? HELP! HELP!
(beginning to cry)

She can be seen tossing her wishing cap across the room later in the movie, after the snowstorm has awakened Dorothy. Only those who have read Baum's book will recognize the Golden Cap with which the Wicked Witch of the West summons her monkeys.

SCARECROW   It's no use screaming at a time like this! Nobody will hear you! HELP! HELP! HELP!

LONG SHOT—TIN MAN AND SCARECROW

in poppy field.

Suddenly the theme music of the GOOD WITCH fades in softly, and the next moment the sky is full of falling snowflakes. Superimposed through this scene we see faintly the face of GLINDA as she waves her wand—to get across the fact that GLINDA has answered their call.

SCARECROW   HELP! HELP! HELP! *(now looking up in wonder)* It's snowing!

CLOSEUP—DOROTHY WITH TOTO IN HER ARMS

asleep, as the snow begins settling on her

LONG SHOT—TIN MAN AND SCARECROW

Superimposed with CLOSEUP of GLINDA as she waves her wand. Snow still falling.

SCARECROW   No, it isn't! Yes, it is! Oh, maybe that'll help! Oh, but it couldn't help!

CLOSEUP—DOROTHY

stirs slightly and opens her eyes.

SCARECROW   Does help! Dorothy, you're waking up!

DOROTHY *(rising)*   Oh . . . oh . . .

LION *(sitting up)*   Ah—ah. Unusual weather we're havin', ain't we?

They laugh.

DOROTHY *(pointing to TIN MAN)*   Look, he's rusted again! Oh, give me the oil can, quick!

SCARECROW *(handing it to her)*   Here! Oh! Here!

DOROTHY *(oiling his joints)*   Oh, quick! Oh!

SCARECROW He is rusted! Here!

DOROTHY Here! Oh! Oh, quick! Oh! Oh!

CLOSEUP—INT. TOWER ROOM

Their images in crystal. CAMERA PULLS back to WITCH and NIKKO as the picture fades.

WITCH *(furiously)* Curseit! Curseit! Somebody always helps that girl! (NIKKO *hands her the wishing cap)* But shoes or no shoes, . . . I'm still great enough to conquer her! And woe to those who try to stop me!
(She flings it furiously across the room.)

LAP DISSOLVE TO:
FULL SHOT—THE FOUR

DOROTHY Come on, let's get out of here. Look—Emerald City is closer and prettier than ever!

They link arms and tramp out of the snow-covered field as they hear a chorus of voices offscreen begin to sing.

OPTIMISTIC VOICES *(out of the air—singing)*
You're out of the woods
You're out of the dark
You're out of the night

Step into the sun
Step into the light
Keep straight ahead for
The most glor . . .
. . . ious place
On the face
Of the earth or the sky

LONG SHOT—THE EMERALD CITY

as they go skipping arm in arm down the Yellow Brick Road.

OPTIMISTIC VOICES *(cont'd.)*
Hold onto your breath
Hold onto your heart

Hold onto your hope
March up to the gate
And bid it open—

LAP DISSOLVE TO:
MEDIUM SHOT—INT. TOWER ROOM—WITCH AND
NIKKO

She grabs her broomstick and laughs, going to window.

WITCH Ha! *(laughing)* To the Emerald City as fast as lightning!

LONG SHOT—EXT. TOWER

CAMERA PANS with WITCH as she flies away on her broomstick,
laughing wildly.

LAP DISSOLVE TO:
LONG SHOT—GATE TO THE EMERALD CITY

The FOUR are skipping up to the gate.

OPTIMISTIC VOICES *(singing)**
You're out of the woods
You're out of the dark
You're out of the night

Step into the sun
Step into the light
March up to the gate
And bid it open!—open!

MEDIUM SHOT—THE FOUR AT THE GATE

* "Optimistic Voices" (or "Choral Sequence to 'Gates of Emerald City' ") was originally a longer number titled "The Land of Oz." On entering the gates, Dorothy and her friends were to be greeted by the chorus, singing:

Behold! You are in the Em'rald City of Oz
We're told that a more enchanted land never was
Behold your dream as it gleams in the sun
Every beam is a jewel that shines for a deed well done
Look high! There's a magic Make-Believe in the air
And oh! If you still can use a dream . . . Take your share!
A more enthralling vision of a wish-come-true never was
So here's to the hearts that believe and belong
In the land of Oz.

DOROTHY rings the bell. A little window in the door opens.

CLOSE SHOT—THE WINDOW

Out pops a head with a round face. Although he now wears a mustache, something about the head is strangely reminiscent of our old friend, PROFESSOR MARVEL.

DOORMAN *(fiercely)* Who rang that bell?

MEDIUM SHOT—THE FOUR

ALL *(together)* We did!

DOORMAN *(still more severely)* Can't you read?

SCARECROW Read what?

DOORMAN The notice!

ALL *(together)* What notice?

DOORMAN It's on the door—as plain as the nose on my face! It's ah —oh—oh—oh—oh.
(He cranes his head out, clucks with annoyance, vanishes, and his hand immediately reappears with a card, which he hangs out of the window, and then slams it shut.)

ALL *(reading card)* "Bell out of order. Please knock."
(DOROTHY then knocks. The window opens once more, and the DOORMAN's face reappears.)

DOORMAN Well, that's more like it! Now, state your business.

ALL *(together)* We want to see the Wizard!

DOORMAN *(so shocked that he almost falls)* Oh—oh—the Wizard? Ah—but nobody can see the Great Oz! Nobody's ever seen the Great Oz! Even *I've* never seen him!

DOROTHY *(guilelessly)* Well, then, how do you know there is one?

DOORMAN Because—he . . . ah . . . b—I—oh—
(unable to think of a good reason)
You're wasting my time!

DOROTHY   Oh, please—please, sir—I've *got* to see the Wizard. The Good Witch of the North sent me.

DOORMAN   Prove it!

SCARECROW   She's wearing the ruby slippers she gave her!

INSERT

of DOROTHY's RUBY SLIPPERS

DOORMAN   Oh, so she is! Well, bust my buttons! Why didn't you say that in the first place? That's a horse of a different color! Come on in! *(slams window)*

LONG SHOT

As they come through the gates, we see the beautiful, glittering streets of Emerald City beyond them. As they enter, a buggy drawn by a WHITE HORSE drives up. Strange as it may seem, the fat CABBY is also PROFESSOR MARVEL, in an entirely different makeup and wearing a scrubby little beard and mustache. In this character he is as cockney as a costermonger.

CABBY   *(as he drives up)*   Cabby! Cabby! Just what you're looking for! Tyke you anywhere in the city, we does!

DOROTHY   *(as he looks down)*   Well, would you take us to see the Wizard?

CABBY   *(stalling)*   The Wizard? The Wizard? . . . I . . . can't . . . well, yes, of course . . . But first I'll tyke you to a little place where you can tidy up a bit, what?

DOROTHY   *(getting in, followed by others)*   Oh, thank you, so much, we've been gone such a long time, and we feel so mess—

CAMERA PANS to HORSE in foreground, showing that it now has turned to a beautiful shade of purple.

DOROTHY   *(to CABBY)*   What kind of a horse is *that*? I've never seen a horse like *that* before!

CABBY   No, and never will again, I fancy! There's only one of him, and he's it. He's the Horse of a Different Color you've heard tell about! *(laughs)*

CABBY starts off. We carry them in a TRUCKING SHOT through the street as the CABBY leads into his song.

CABBY AND CITIZENS *(singing)*
Ha-ha-ha
Ho-ho-ho
And a couple of tra-la-las
That's how we laugh the day away
In the Merry Old Land of Oz
'Bzz-'bzz-'bzz
Chirp, chirp, chirp
And a couple of la-de-das.
(The HORSE *neighs and is now red.)*
That's how the crickets crick all day
In the Merry Old Land of Oz.
We get up at twelve and start to work at one,
(The HORSE *neighs and is now yellow)*
Take an hour for lunch, and then at two we're done,
Jolly good fun.

Ha-ha-ha!
Ho-ho-ho!
And a couple of tra-la-las,
That's how we laugh the day away,
In the Merry Old Land of Oz.
Ha-ha-ha
Ho-ho-ho

CABBY
Ha-ha-ha-ha!

CITIZENS
And a couple of tra-la-las

ALL
That's how we laugh the day away,
With a ho-ho-ho!
Ha-ha-ha!
In the Merry Old Land of Oz.

We synchronize end of song with arrival of CARRIAGE in front of the magic washup parlor, with "Wash & Brush Up Co." over the door.

MUSICAL MONTAGE. As the four get down, we go into a short musical montage (still using the song with a few new lines to point up the scenes).

The first eight bars are taken up by the MASSEURS, who are filling the SCARECROW with new straw.

MASSEURS *(singing)*
Pat, pat here,
Pat, pat there,
And a couple of brand-new strahz. *
That's how we keep you young and fair
In the Merry Old Land of Oz.

POLISHERS shining up the TIN MAN.

POLISHERS *(singing)*
Rub, rub here,
Rub, rub there,
And whether you're tin or brahz.
That's how we keep you in repair
In the Merry Old Land of Oz.

DOROTHY at the BEAUTICIANS'.

BEAUTICIAN *(singing)*
We can make a dimpled smile out of a frown.

DOROTHY
Can you even dye my eyes to match my gown?

BEAUTICIAN
Uh-huh.

DOROTHY
Jolly old town!

---

* Harburg noted on his manuscript, "People in Oz rhyme all *aws* sounds with *Oz*."

MANICURISTS fixing LION's claws . . .

MANICURISTS *(singing)*
> *Clip, clip here,*
> *Clip, clip there,*
> *We give the roughest clawzz—*

LION *(singing)*
> *That certain air of savoir faire*
> *In the Merry Old Land of Oz!—Ha!*

The other three join him, all laughing.

SCARECROW
> *Ha-ha-ha-*

TIN MAN
> *Ho-ho-ho-*

DOROTHY
> *Ha-ha-ha-ha-*

LION *(rising)*
> *Ha!*

ALL *(singing)*
> *That's how we laugh the day away*
> *In the Merry Old Land of Oz*
> *(As all* FOUR *are coming out into the City Square, the whole town is singing.)*
> *That's how we laugh the day away*
> *And a ha-ha-ha*
> *Ha-ha-ha-ha-ha-ha*
> *Ha-ha-ha-ha-ha-ha-ha-ha-ha-*
> *In the Merry Old Land of Oz*
> *Ha-ha-ha-ho-ho-ho—(laughing)*

THE FOUR
> *We're off to see the Wizard*
> *The Wonderful Wizard of—*

There is a LOUD NOISE. All stop and look up, screaming.

LONG SHOT—SKY OVER CITY

The WITCH is flying overhead on her broomstick. She laughs as a long streak of black smoke trails out from behind and forms the letters: S—U—R—R

MEDIUM SHOT—FOUR

looking up.

LION   Who's her? Who's her?

DOROTHY   It's the Witch! She's followed us here!

LONG SHOT—SKY

In smoke the WITCH has written:
SURRENDER DOROTHY

LION   "Surrender Dorothy."

DOROTHY   Oh!

OZ WOMAN NO. 1   Dorothy? Who's Dorothy!

OZ WOMAN NO. 2   The Wizard will explain it!

OZ MAN NO. 1   To the Wizard!

OZ MAN NO. 2   To the Wizard!

They are all rushing off.

DOROTHY   Dear, whatever shall we do?

SCARECROW   Well, we'd better hurry if we're going to see the Wizard!

They run off with the rest of the crowd.

LONG SHOT—THE GATES OF THE PALACE

This is in front of the Palace of Oz, where there are flowers and steps going up to double doors. A crowd of townspeople is surrounding the gates, clamoring to see the Wizard.

In front of the gates stands a funny GUARD, dressed in a tall shako and a costume that is a slightly exaggerated version of the English palace guards. He carries an extremely long gun with flowers in the barrel. Believe it or not, the GUARD is PROFESSOR MARVEL, with a fiercely turned-up mustache.

GUARD *(bellowing at the mob)* Here—here! Here! Everything is all right. Stop that now—just—every—it's all right! Everything is all right! The Great and Powerful Oz has got matters well in hand—I hope—and so you can all go home! And there's nothing to worry about! Get out of here now—go on! Go on home, and I—I—Go home.

DOROTHY and HER FRIENDS make their way through the crowd.

DOROTHY If you please, sir—we want to see the Wizard right away —all four of us!

GUARD *(firmly)* Orders are: Nobody can see the Great Oz, not nobody, not nohow!

DOROTHY Oh, but—but please. It's very important.

LION And—and I got a permanent just for the occasion.

GUARD Not nobody, not nohow!*

SCARECROW But she's Dorothy!

GUARD The Witch's Dorothy? Humph! Well, that makes a difference! Just wait here—I'll announce you at once!
(He marches inside.)

* Here a comic changing of the Wizard's guard was shot and then cut from the movie:

A BUGLE SOUNDS.

GUARD *(looking quickly over his shoulder)* Beg pardon—we've got to change the Guards.
(He marches importantly into the sentry house and turns around. The mustache, which turned fiercely skyward, is now turned equally fiercely downward. He marches out again.)

(bellowing)
Now what do *you* want?

ALL *(in astonishment)* We want to see the Wizard of Oz.

GUARD Not nobody, not nohow!

TIN MAN That's what the other man said.

SCARECROW   Did you hear that? He'll announce us at once! I've as good as got my brain!

TIN MAN   I can fairly hear my heart beating!

DOROTHY   I'll be home in time for supper!

LION   In another hour I'll be King of the Forest. Long live the King!
(singing)
If I were King of the Forest,
Not Queen, not Duke, not Prince.
My regal robes of the forest
Would be satin, not cotton, not chintz.
I'd command each thing, be it fish or fowl,
With a woof and a woof, and a royal growl—woof.
As I'd click my heel,
All the trees would kneel,
And the mountains bow,
And the bulls kowtow,
And the sparrow would take wing
'F—I . . . 'f . . . I . . . were King.

Each rabbit would show respect to me.
The chipmunks genuflect to me.
Though my tail would lash,
I would show compash
For every underling,
'F—I . . . 'f . . . I . . . were King—
Just King. *

Coronation ceremony to music. Business of laying down carpet,

* Some additional lyrics were deleted from the final film:

ALL *(together)*
The rabbits would show respect to him
The chipmunks genuflect to him

SCARECROW
His wife would be Queen of the May.

LION
I'd be monarch of all I survey.

These cuts were restored, however, when the number was performed by Lahr and other cast members on the NBC radio program *Maxwell House Good News,* on June 29, 1939.

DOROTHY acting as flower girl and train bearer picking up rug as a royal robe, and the TIN MAN breaking a flowerpot and crowning the LION with it.

LION *(singing)*
Monarch of all I survey
Mah-ah-ah-ah-ah-ah-ah-ah-ah-narch!
Of all I survey!

DOROTHY and the SCARECROW bow.

DOROTHY   Your Majesty, if you were King
You wouldn't be afraid of anything?

LION   Not nobody, not nohow!

TIN MAN   Not even a rhinocerous?

LION   Imposserous!

DOROTHY   How about a hippopotamus!

LION   Why, I'd thrash him from top to bottomus.

DOROTHY   Supposin' you met an elephant!

LION   I'd wrap him up in cellophant.

SCARECROW   What if it were a brontosaurus?

LION   I'd show him who was King of the Fores'.

ALL   How?

LION
How? . . . Courage!
What makes a king out of a slave!
. . . Courage!
What makes the flag on the mast to wave!
. . . Courage!
What makes the elephant charge his tusk
In the misty mist or the dusky dusk?
What makes the muskrat guard his musk?
. . . Courage!

What makes the sphinx the seventh wonder?
. . . Courage!
What makes the dawn come up like thunder?
. . . Courage!
What makes the Hottentot so hot?
What puts the "ape" in apricot?
What have they got that I ain't got?

ALL   Courage!

LION   You can say that again! Ha, ha—huh?*

LONG SHOT—DOOR

The GUARD comes out of the Palace.

GUARD   Ahhhhh! The Wizard says go away!
(exits, slamming door)

ALL *(in horror)*   Go *away*?

DOROTHY   Oh—

SCARECROW *(mildly)*   Looks like we came a long way for nothing.

DOROTHY *(really losing her courage for the first time)*   Oh, and I was
so happy—*(sits down on the steps.)* I thought I was on my way
home.

As she begins to cry, the others all start comforting her. The

* The number went on to the following finish, dropped from the final film:
LION
   For courage is the thing of kings
   With courage I'd be king of kings
   And the whole year round I'd be hailed and crowned
   By every living thing
   'F—I . . .
ALL
   'F—he . . .
LION
   'F—I . . .
ALL
   'F—he . . .
LION
   . . . were king!

SCARECROW takes the handkerchief from her basket and hands it to her.

As she talks brokenly, the GUARD is peering out the window in the door. He is beginning to be affected by the scene.

TIN MAN Don't cry, Dorothy. We're going to get you to the Wizard.

SCARECROW We certainly are.

DOROTHY *(who has been growing more and more unhappy)* Auntie Em was so good to me, and I never appreciated it . . . running away and hurting her feelings. Professor Marvel said she was sick. She may be dying! And it's all my fault.

CLOSEUP—GUARD AT WINDOW

Tears trickle down his cheeks and drip off his mustache.

DOROTHY Oh, I'll never forgive myself! Never—never—never!

GUARD *(sobbing)* Oh, oh! Please don't cry anymore! I'll get you in to the Wizard somehow! Come on. I had an Aunt Em myself once.

He disappears, and the doors of the Palace open slowly. The four enter down a long corridor.

LONG SHOT—INT. PALACE CORRIDOR

It seems to stretch on forever, high and narrow, and has an awe-inspiring air of mystery and silence. DOROTHY, the TIN MAN, the SCARECROW, and the LION are walking down this corridor slowly, cautiously.

LION *(stopping)* Wait a minute, fellas! I was just thinkin'—I really don't want to see the Wizard this much. I better wait for you outside.

He turns to go, but they stop him.

SCARECROW What's the matter?

TIN MAN Oh, he's just ascared again.

DOROTHY *(reassuringly)* Don't you know the Wizard's going to give you some courage?

LION *(twiddling his tail nervously, occasionally wiping away tears with the brush on the end)* I'd be too scared to ask him for it! *(bawling)*

DOROTHY Oh, well, then we'll ask him *for* you!

LION I'd sooner wait outside.

He turns to run, but they stop him.

DOROTHY Why? Why?

LION *(sobbing)* Because I'm still scared!

DOROTHY Come on.

LION *(absently tugs at his tail with his paws and gives a wail of fear)* Ow-oo!

SCARECROW *(as they turn)* What happened?

LION *(bawling)* Somebody pulled my tail!

SCARECROW You did it yourself!

LION *(looking at his paws)* I—oh—

SCARECROW Here . . . come on.

They all clasp hands. *

* The shooting script here includes an amusing scene not in the final film:

> *All FOUR link hands and tiptoe four paces down the passage and then stop. The echo of their four steps comes back at them loud and clear.*

LION What was that?

DOROTHY Our echo.

LION'S ECHO Tap-tap-tap-tap— What was that?—that?—that?

DOROTHY'S ECHO Our echo—echo—echo.
> *The LION turns around and tries to run, and they hold him fast and advance along the passage with CAMERA TRUCKING with them. TRUCK CLOSE SHOT—The pillars along the walls are decorated with huge carved faces that look down on the four.*

> CLOSE SHOT—FOUR

> *The LION stops again.*

DOROTHY *(in a whisper)* Oh, come on, come on—we'll soon find the Wizard!

OZ'S VOICE *(booming and echoing)* Come forward!

LONG SHOT—END OF CORRIDOR

Two huge doors swing open.

LONG SHOT—FOUR

walking cautiously forward

LION *(clasping his paws over his eyes)* Tell me when it's over!

*LONG SHOT—INT. THRONE ROOM—SHOOTING FROM
THEIR ANGLE*

It is a huge, lofty hall, beautifully decorated in green and silver glass. At the far end is a short flight of stairs leading to a huge throne. On the steps also are two silver urns, from which flames and smoke arise. A gigantic, shadowy head hovers above the throne.

LION Look at that! Look at that! *(crying)* I want to go home!

OZ'S VOICE: I am Oz, the Great and Powerful! Who are you? . . .

LONG SHOT—FOUR

They are huddled together in an unhappy little group. The LION is shivering. The rest are nudging DOROTHY, indicating that she is to be the spokesperson. In the end they shove her forward.

OZ'S VOICE: *Who are you?*

DOROTHY I—if you please, I am Dorothy, the Small and Meek. We've come to ask you—

LONG SHOT—THRONE

Flame and smoke pouring out.

OZ'S VOICE *(booming forth and interrupting)* SILENCE!

DOROTHY *(running back)* Oh! Oh! Jiminy Crickets!

DOROTHY'S ECHO *(faintly)* The Wizard! The Wizard!
(louder—the tone and pitch change)
The Great and Powerful Wizard of Oz!!!! *Oz!! Oz!! Oz!! Oz!!! Oz!!! Oz!!! Oz!!!*

OZ'S VOICE   The Great and Powerful Oz knows *why* you have come! Step forward, *Tin Man!*

TIN MAN *(trembling so hard his joints rattle, is shoved forward by DOROTHY)*   Ohhhh!

OZ'S VOICE   You dare to come to me for a heart—do you? You clinking, clanking, clattering collection of caliginous junk!

TIN MAN   Ohhh—yes . . . yes, sir—y-y-yes, Your Honor. You see, a while back, we were walking down the Yellow Brick Road, and—

OZ'S VOICE   Quiet!

TIN MAN *(running back to the others)*   Ohhhh!

OZ'S VOICE   And *you,* Scarecrow, have the effrontery to ask for a brain? You billowing bale of bovine fodder!

SCARECROW *(salaaming before throne)*   Y-yes—Yes, Your Honor— I mean, Your Excellency—I—I mean—Your *Wizardry!*

OZ'S VOICE   Enough!

The SCARECROW returns to his companions.

OZ'S VOICE   Uhhh—and *you,* Lion!

The LION groans with fear as he is slowly pushed forward.

OZ'S VOICE   *Well!*

CLOSE ON LION

He begins to speak and faints dead away. The others run to him.

DOROTHY straightens up from LION and turns on WIZARD.

DOROTHY *(angrily)*   Oh—oh! You ought to be *ashamed* of yourself! Frightening him like that, when he came to you for help!

OZ'S VOICE   *Silence,* whippersnapper!

DOROTHY sits down suddenly.

OZ'S VOICE *(cont'd.)* The beneficent Oz has every intention of granting your requests!

CLOSER ON GROUP

as the LION comes out of his faint and sits up.

DOROTHY   What?

LION *(full of excitement)*   What's that? What'd he say?

DOROTHY *(pulling him up)*   Oh, come on.

LION *(getting to his feet)*   Huh? What'd he say?

OZ'S VOICE   But first you must prove yourselves worthy by performing a very small task. Bring me the broomstick of the Witch of the West!

TIN MAN   B-b-b-b-but if we do that, we'd have to kill her to get it!

OZ'S VOICE   Bring me her broomstick and I'll grant your requests! Now go!

LION   But—but what if she kills us first?

OZ'S VOICE   I said *GO!*

LONG SHOT—FOUR

The LION gives a wailing moan. CAMERA PANS as he turns and runs like mad out of the throne room and into the corridor.

LONG SHOT—CORRIDOR

The LION comes running forward. CAMERA PANS as he turns and dives through the window with a crash.

FADE OUT:

FADE IN ON:
HAUNTED FOREST
CRANE TRUCK SHOT

to weird, tremolo music. The CAMERA pushes downward through a bunch of leafy branches in a very creepy-looking wood. Now it TRUCKS to a signpost:
        HAUNTED FOREST

WITCHES CASTLE
1 MILE

Beneath this is:

I'D TURN
BACK IF I
WERE YOU!

LAP DISSOLVE TO:
LONG SHOT—FOUR

The SCARECROW carries a water pistol and a stick that bends like rubber in the middle. The TIN MAN carries a huge wrench, and the LION carries a fish net and a spray pump with "WITCH RE-MOVER" printed on it. They stop and look at signpost.

LION   "I'd Turn Back If I Were You."
(He nods and deliberately turns around to start back, but the others stop him. He growls as they proceed.)

CLOSE SHOT—TWO BLACK OWLS

with illuminated eyes, gazing down from a tree.

MEDIUM SHOT—FOUR

The LION turns to run, but the TIN MAN and SCARECROW at once link their arms firmly in his and turn him back to face the right way, swinging him quickly into the air, however, so that his legs pedal madly in space, all the time crying.

LION *(bawling)*   Oh, look! Look! Oh, look . . . !

CLOSE UP—TWO CROWS

blinking their red eyes, in another tree. *

---

* The shooting script contains a short scene dropped from the movie that inspires their fear of spooks in the Haunted Forest:

TIN MAN *(in a whisper)*   From now on, we're on enemy ground.
(to DOROTHY)
You should have *something* to *protect* yourself with.

LION *(quickly)*   She—she can have my "Witch Remover"!

DOROTHY *(doubtfully)*   Does it work?

LION *(crestfallen)*   No, but it's wonderful for threatening with!

SCARECROW   I believe there're spooks around here.

TIN MAN *(trying to be bold)*   That's ridiculous! Spooks! That's silly!

LION   D-don't you believe in spooks?

TIN MAN   No! Why, on—Oh!

TRICK SHOT

The TIN MAN suddenly vanishes straight up.

DOROTHY   Oh! Oh! Tin Man! Oh! Oh!

He suddenly reappears a few yards farther along the path as he hits the ground with a deafening crash.

DOROTHY   Oh—oh—

SCARECROW   Oh, are you—are you all right?

As the SCARECROW and DOROTHY run forward to help him, the LION remains and repeats to himself in an earnest, anxious voice.

LION *(trembling with eyes closed)*   I do believe in spooks, I do believe in spooks; I do, I do, I do, I do, I do I . . .

MEDIUM SHOT—INT. TOWER ROOM

The WITCH watching the image of the LION in her crystal with NIKKO and other WINGED MONKEYS.

LION   . . . do believe in spooks; I do believe in spooks; I do, I do, I do, I do, I do, I do! *(then fades)*

DOROTHY   Oh—

SCARECROW   Oh, here— Gimme that thing!

He takes the "WITCH REMOVER" spray and throws it away.

CLOSE SHOT—THE SPRAY

As it hits the ground, it vanishes.

MEDIUM SHOT—FOUR

They watch, fascinated, and then look at each other.

SCARECROW *(awed)*   Did you see that?

OTHER THREE   Yes.

WITCH *(laughing)* You'll believe in more than that before I've finished with you!

CAMERA PANS as she rises and goes to the window, addressing the WINGED MONKEYS.

WITCH Take your army to the Haunted Forest and bring me that girl and her dog. Do what you like with the others, but I want her alive and unharmed! They'll give you no trouble, I promise you that. I've sent a little insect on ahead to take the fight out of them! Ha, ha, ha, ha, ha, ha! Take special care of those ruby slippers—I want those most of all! *(By now the WINGED MONKEYS are flying past the window screaming and chattering, so that the WITCH has to shout to make herself heard.)*
Now fly—fly! Fly! Fly! Fly!

CAMERA PULLS BACK as the WITCH stands by the window, silhouetted against the sky with her batlike army passing by.

LAP DISSOLVE TO:*
LONG SHOT—SKY

The WINGED MONKEYS come flying toward the CAMERA in flight formation.

MEDIUM SHOT—HAUNTED FOREST

The FOUR look up in the sky in terror. The WINGED MONKEYS swoop down on them.

Two run after DOROTHY.

DOROTHY Help! Help! Help!

As the TIN MAN swings his ax, the MONKEYS capture him.

TIN MAN Go 'way now! Or I'll—I'll . . .

Other MONKEYS tromp on the SCARECROW.

SCARECROW Help! Help! Oh! Oh!

The two MONKEYS grab DOROTHY.

* See Appendix C: The Jitterbug, pp. 138–141.

DOROTHY   Toto! Toto! Help, Toto!

CLOSEUP—TOTO

looks up after DOROTHY, barking.

LONG SHOT—HAUNTED FOREST

DOROTHY screams as she is carried over the trees.

Another MONKEY grabs TOTO and disappears.

GROUP SHOT AT SCARECROW

who is lying on the ground as the WINGED MONKEYS fly off. The TIN MAN and LION come over to help him.

SCARECROW   Help! Help! Help!

TIN MAN   Oh, well, what happened to you?

SCARECROW   They tore my legs off and they threw them over there. Then they took my chest out and then they threw it over there—

TIN MAN   Well—that's you all over.

LION   They sure knocked the stuffin's out of ya, didn't they?

SCARECROW   Don't stand there talking! Put me together! We've got to find Dorothy!

TIN MAN   Now, let's see . . .

LAP DISSOLVE TO:
LONG SHOT—WITCH'S CASTLE

perched high atop a mountainous rock.

LAP DISSOLVE TO:
CLOSE SHOT—INT. WITCH'S CASTLE
WITCH'S TOWER ROOM

The WITCH is talking to TOTO in her lap.

WITCH *(with diabolical sweetness)*   What a nice little dog. *(puts him in the basket and hands it to NIKKO)* And you, my dear, what an unexpected pleasure. It's so kind of you to visit me in my loneliness.

DOROTHY *(in great distress)* What are you going to do with my dog? Give him back to me!

WITCH All in good time, my little pretty, all in good time.

DOROTHY Oh, please, give me back my dog!

WITCH Certainly—certainly. When *you* give *me* those slippers.

DOROTHY But the Good Witch of the North told me not to!

WITCH Very well! *(savagely to* NIKKO*)* Throw that basket in the river and drown him!

DOROTHY *(frantic)* No! No—no! Here—you can *have* your old slippers, but give me back Toto!

WITCH *(elated)* That's a good little girl! I knew you'd see reason! *(She stoops down impatiently.)*

INSERT (TRICK SHOT)—CLOSEUP OF WITCH'S HANDS

grabbing at the RUBY SLIPPERS. They suddenly flash like red fire. The WITCH shrieks with pain.

BACK TO SCENE

The WITCH shrinks back, staring at her hands and down at the slippers.

WITCH Ohhhh! Ohhhh!

DOROTHY I'm sorry. I didn't do it.

WITCH Oh!

DOROTHY Can I still have my dog?

WITCH *(savagely)* No! Fool that I am! I should have remembered! Those slippers will never come off . . . as long as you're alive! *(in a silky voice)*
But that's not what's worrying me . . . it's *how* to do it . . . these things must be done delicately, or you hurt the spell . . .

CLOSE SHOT—BASKET

TOTO suddenly pushes his head out and scrambles out and across the floor and out the door.

DOROTHY   Run, Toto, run!

WITCH *(furiously to* NIKKO*)*   Catch him, you fool!

LONG SHOT—INT. HALLWAY

TOTO comes tearing down the steps.

LONG SHOT—EXT. DRAWBRIDGE

TOTO comes flying out of the castle just as the drawbridge begins to rise.

CLOSEUP—TOTO AT THE EDGE OF RISING DRAW-BRIDGE

He hesitates for a moment.

LONG SHOT—DRAWBRIDGE

As the WINKIES *rush out of the castle, carrying long spears,* TOTO *jumps from the bridge and lands among the rocks on the other side.*

DOROTHY   Run, Toto, run!

The WINKIES *miss* TOTO *when they throw their spears, and he runs off through the rocks.*

DOROTHY   Run, Toto! Run!

CLOSE SHOT—DOROTHY AT WINDOW

DOROTHY *(cont'd.) (joyfully)*   He got away! He got away!

WITCH *(savagely)*   Ohhhh! *(*DOROTHY *turns back from window in fear.)* Which is more than you will! Drat you and your dog! You've been more trouble to me than you're worth, one way and another, but it'll soon be over now!
(She seizes a large hourglass off the table and holds it up and turns it over.)
You see that? That's how much longer you've got to be alive.

(DOROTHY cries.) And it isn't long, my pretty, it isn't long! I can't wait forever to get those shoes!
(The WITCH *goes out of the door and slams and locks it shut.)*

CLOSEUP—THE HOURGLASS

with the sand running through.

MEDIUM SHOT—DOROTHY

CAMERA PANS as DOROTHY moves over to the throne and sits down by the crystal.

DOROTHY *(sobbing)*   I'm frightened—I'm frightened, Auntie Em—I'm frightened!

TRICK SHOT—CRYSTAL

just beside DOROTHY begins to swirl and smoke restlessly; and then AUNT EM DISSOLVES IN:

AUNT EM *(calling)*   Dorothy . . . Dorothy, where are you? It's me— It's Auntie Em . . . we're trying to find you . . . where are you?

DOROTHY *(sobbing)*   I'm here in Oz, Auntie Em! I'm locked up in the Witch's castle . . . and I'm trying to get home to you, Auntie Em!
*(*AUNT EM*'s face has begun to fade from the crystal, having made no sign of hearing* DOROTHY*.)*
Oh, Auntie Em—don't go away! I'm frightened! Come back! Come back!

The WITCH's face suddenly appears in the crystal instead. DOROTHY shrinks back from the crystal in terror.

WITCH *(mimicking* DOROTHY*)*   Auntie Em, Auntie Em! Come back! I'll give you Auntie Em, my pretty! *(She laughs.)**

CLOSEUP—THE HOURGLASS

with the sand running through.

---

* See Appendix E: The Rainbow Bridge, pp. 144–151.

LAP DISSOLVE TO:
IN A SERIES OF QUICK CUTS

we show TOTO making his way down to the bottom of the rocks and rushing through the forest, barking.

MEDIUM SHOT—CLEARING WHERE DOROTHY WAS SEIZED

The TIN MAN and the LION are busy stuffing odd strands of straw into the SCARECROW, who lies on the ground. TOTO rushes into the clearing, barking furiously.

TIN MAN   Look! There's Toto! Where'd he come from?

SCARECROW   Why, don't you see? He's come to take us to Dorothy!

TIN MAN   Oh—

SCARECROW   Come on, fellas!

TOTO barks and leads them down the trail.

LAP DISSOLVE TO:
LONG SHOT—HILLSIDE

where the COWARDLY LION is fighting his way over the boulders and slippery shale, with the TIN MAN holding onto his tail. The SCARECROW is coming up from behind.

The TIN MAN slips, hanging on to the LION's tail to keep from falling.

LION   I—I—I hope my strength holds out.

TIN MAN   I hope your *tail* holds out! Oh!*

LONG SHOT—WITCH'S CASTLE

* Cut from the final film was another scene of Dorothy in the Witch's tower room. As the sand is running through the hourglass, she runs to one door and then to another, but both are locked. She begins sobbing, then sings:

Someday I'll wake and rub my eyes
And in that land beyond the skies
You'll find me—

She breaks down and sobs by the Witch's crystal.

This shows the great towers of the castle silhouetted against the sky on the peak of the mountain. There is a full moon that makes it almost bright as day.

CLOSEUP—THE ROCKS

The THREE appear out of the rocks.

LION What's that? What's that?

LONG SHOT—THE TOWER OF THE WITCH'S CASTLE

CLOSE SHOT—THE THREE

SCARECROW That's the castle of the Wicked Witch! Dorothy's in that awful place?

TIN MAN Oh, I hate to think of her in there. We've got to get her out! *(begins crying)*

SCARECROW Don't cry now. We haven't got the oil can with us, and you've been squeaking enough as it is!

LION Who's them? Who's them?

LONG SHOT—ENTRANCE TO CASTLE

(as seen by the group) guarded by a dozen enormous WINKIE GUARDS holding wicked-looking weapons.

WINKIES *(chanting as they march)*
    O—Ee—Yah! Eoh—Ah!
    O—Ee—Yah! Eoh—Ah!
    O—Ee—Yah! Eoh—Ah! . . .

CLOSE SHOT—THE ROCKS

SCARECROW I've got a plan how to get in there . . .

LION Fine. He's got a plan.

SCARECROW . . . and you're gonna lead us.

LION Yeah—Me?

SCARECROW Yes, you.

LION I—I—I gotta get her outta there?

SCARECROW That's right.

LION All right, I'll go in there for Dorothy—Wicked Witch or no Wicked Witch—guards or no guards—I'll tear 'em apart—Woof! I may not come out alive, but I'm goin' in there! There's only one thing I want you fellas to do.

SCARECROW and TIN MAN What's that?

LION Talk me out of it!
(He starts to turn, but the OTHERS stop him.)

TIN MAN No, you don't!

SCARECROW Oh, no!

LION No? Now wait a minute!

TIN MAN Get up here—

They push him forward.

SCARECROW Up!

LION Now . . .

LAP DISSOLVE TO:
CLOSEUP—THE HOURGLASS

with the sand running through.

LAP DISSOLVE TO:
MEDIUM SHOT—NEAR ROCK

They watch the WINKIE GUARDS marching. TOTO barks. They indicate for him to be silent.

The towering helmets of three huge WINKIE GUARDS rise above them behind the rocks. These are not seen by the group.

They are whispering to each other. By now the GUARDS have dropped down behind them. The LION turns and sees them. He tries to speak but cannot. He tries to get their attention, but they shush him.

The GUARDS pounce on them, and all vanish behind the rocks, from which comes a yelling and a thumping.

LION Put 'em up!

LAP DISSOLVE TO:
CLOSEUP—THE ROCKS

The sounds of the fray die down. One by one, three Winkie helmets appear above the rocks. We feel the WINKIES have vanquished, if not killed, Dorothy's friends. As they come up from below the rock, the first two are the TIN MAN and SCARECROW in the heavy Winkie uniforms, and the third is the LION with his tail wagging in the air. TOTO emerges with a piece of tassel in his teeth.

LONG SHOT—ENTRANCE

as the WINKIE GUARDS march up, chanting.

SCARECROW Come on, I've got another idea.

LION Do—do ya think it'll be polite, droppin' in like this?

SCARECROW and TIN MAN Come on . . . come on.

They move through the rocks.

CLOSER ON ENTRANCE

Our THREE FRIENDS march in the picture, then goose-step through the entrance into the castle after the WINKIE GUARDS. The last one is the LION, who is having a dreadful time with his tail. TOTO is bringing up the rear of the procession as the drawbridge is pulled up.

LONG SHOT—INT. CASTLE—ENTRANCE HALL

As they reach across hall, the WINKIE GUARDS turn smartly and march off. Our THREE duck behind a partition in the wall.

TIN MAN Where do we go now?

LION Yeah!

TOTO barks on steps.

SCARECROW *(pointing at* TOTO*)* There!

They run up the stairs after TOTO.

LONG SHOT—UPPER HALLWAY

This is outside the door to the Witch's tower room.

TOTO barks and then shuffles and scratches at a door.

SCARECROW Wait! We'd better make sure. Dorothy? Are you in there?

LION It's us!

MEDIUM SHOT—INT. TOWER ROOM

DOROTHY *(runs to the door excitedly)* Yes, it's me! She's locked me in!

MEDIUM SHOT—TIN MAN, SCARECROW, AND LION

LION *(excitedly)* Listen, fellas! It's her! We gotta get her out! Open the door!

They discard their spears and uniforms.

LONG SHOT—DOROTHY

DOROTHY Oh, hurry! Please, hurry! . . .

CLOSEUP—THE HOURGLASS

with the sand running through.

DOROTHY *(with renewed urgency)* . . . The hourglass is almost empty!

CLOSE SHOT—DOOR

TIN MAN *(suddenly)* Stand back!
(He begins chopping at the door.)

DOROTHY stands back and picks up basket.

CLOSEUP—THE HOURGLASS

A few grains remain.

IN A SERIES OF QUICK CUTS

the TIN MAN breaks in the door with his chopper.

DOROTHY rushes out and into their arms. The SCARECROW hands her TOTO.

DOROTHY Oh—oh—oh, Toto! Toto! Oh, Lion darling—I knew you'd come!

TIN MAN Dorothy!

DOROTHY I knew you would!

SCARECROW Hurry—we've got no time to lose!

They grab DOROTHY and run down the corridor.

LONG SHOT—STAIRS

The castle is deserted. CAMERA PANS as they run down the stairs and across the hall toward the entrance doors, which are open wide.

Just as they are reaching the doors, with a deafening crash the doors slam shut.

MEDIUM SHOT—OF THE FOUR

beating at the doors and trying to open them. The TIN MAN raises his ax to chop. They swing back in terror, as a burst of wild and savage laughter fills the hall.

CLOSE SHOT—WITCH AND NIKKO

looking down from top of stairs.

WITCH Going so soon? I wouldn't hear of it! Why, my little party's just beginning!

MEDIUM SHOT—FOUR

LION Trapped! Trapped like mice—*(correcting himself)*—er—rats!

LONG SHOT—TOP OF STAIRS

The WITCH holds the empty hourglass triumphantly, laughing.

CAMERA PANS down as about thirty or forty WINKIES pour into the hall.

CLOSEUP—TOTO

MEDIUM SHOT—WINKIES form in a wide half circle, surrounding DOROTHY and her FRIENDS with their spears pointing toward them.

LONG SHOT—SHOOTING DIRECTLY DOWN FROM CEILING

showing the circle of WINKIES closing in on them, step by step.

CLOSE SHOT—WITCH AND NIKKO

WITCH *(laughs)* That's right. Don't hurt them right away. We'll let them *think* about it a little first . . . *(laughs)*

CLOSEUP—SCARECROW

who is thinking hard. He looks up at chandelier and sees a rope, which is tied to a hook in the wall.

CLOSE SHOT—WITCH AND NIKKO

at top of the stairs. She screams and flings down the hourglass, which explodes like a bomb in a flash of red smoke.

CLOSE SHOT—FOUR

The SCARECROW suddenly jerks the TIN MAN's arm, so the ax comes down and cuts the rope fixed to the wall.

LONG SHOT—SHOOTING DOWN

A huge circular iron candelabra with flaming candles gives way and falls on the WINKIES.

CLOSE SHOT—WITCH

She sees what has happened.

WITCH *(cont'd.) (shrieking)* Seize them! Seize them! Stop them, you fools! . . .

LONG SHOT—FOUR

The SCARECROW grabs DOROTHY's hand and runs through the break in the WINKIE line, with the TIN MAN and LION close at his heels.

LONG SHOT—STAIRS

The WITCH and NIKKO run down the stairs after them.

WITCH *(cont'd.)* . . . Stop them! Seize them! Seize them!

LONG SHOT—HALL

The FOUR go rushing into the courtyard, followed by the WINKIES.

The FOUR hide on the other side of a pillar and double back in and run through the hall. They run up the stairs.

The WITCH follows with the WINKIES.

WITCH   There they go! Ah! Now we've got them! Half you go this way—half you go that way! Hurry! Hurry!

The FOUR reach the top of the stairs.

LONG SHOT—CASTLE FROM ABOVE

showing the towers, joined by narrow battlements and a wild mountain river flowing past one side. The FOUR come out of the first tower and onto the battlements, and run along it to the second tower.

LONG SHOT—FOUR

as they halt in the second tower.

LION   Where do we go now?

SCARECROW   This way—Come on!

They run from the second tower.

LONG SHOT—CASTLE FROM ABOVE

as they stop at the stairs leading to the tower.

LONG SHOT—WINKIES

running toward them from the tower.

CLOSE SHOT—FOUR

DOROTHY screams.

SCARECROW *(pointing)* Back! Back!

They run the other way back into the tower.

LONG SHOT—BATTLEMENTS OF CASTLE

as WINKIES enter the tower through both sides.

MEDIUM SHOT—FOUR

as they pull up short. DOROTHY screams. The LION groans. They are all terrorized as the WINKIES trap them in the tower.

LONG SHOT—INT. TOWER

The WITCH enters, followed by NIKKO.

WITCH *(laughing)* Well! Ring-around-the-rosy! A pocketful of spears! Thought you'd be pretty foxy, didn't cha? Well, the last to go will see the first three go before her . . . *(laughs; the FOUR tremble)* . . . and her mangy little dog, too!

CLOSE SHOT—WITCH

grins and looks up. CAMERA PANS as she lifts her broom to a burning torch on the wall. The FOUR tremble.

WITCH *(cont'd.)* How about a little fire, Scarecrow!

MEDIUM SHOT—FOUR

as the WITCH thrusts the blazing broom at the SCARECROW. It sets his arm on fire.

SCARECROW *(jumping up and down)* Oh! No! No!
(DOROTHY *screams)*

SCARECROW *(cont'd.)* Help! I'm burning! I'm burning! I'm burning! Help! Help! Help! Help!

In defense of the SCARECROW, DOROTHY looks around and

suddenly sees a bucket of water. She puts TOTO down and seizes the bucket.

WITCH *(screaming)*   Don't touch that water!

DOROTHY flings its contents toward the SCARECROW.

CLOSEUP—WITCH

as the water hits her full in the face. It puts out the fire.

LONG SHOT—FOUR, WITCH, ETC.

She screams in agony as she shrinks and shrivels.

WITCH   Ohhh! You cursed brat! Look what you've done! I'm melting! Melting! Oh, what a world! What a world! Who would have thought a good little girl like you could destroy my beautiful wickedness! Ohhh! Look out! Look out! I'm going! Ohhhh—Ohhhhhh-hhhh!

CLOSE ON DOROTHY, TIN MAN, SCARECROW, ETC.

look down in amazement.

CLOSEUP—WITCH

who is now no more than her cloak and hat smoldering on the floor.

TOTO paws at it. NIKKO looks on and claps.

LEADER OF THE WINKIES   She's—she's dead. You've killed her.

DOROTHY   I didn't mean to kill her—really I didn't—it's . . . it's just that he was on fire!

LEADER   Hail to Dorothy! The Wicked Witch is dead!

WINKIES *(all drop to their knees before DOROTHY)*   Hail! Hail to Dorothy! The Wicked Witch is dead!

DOROTHY   The broom! May we have it?

LEADER *(handing it to her)*   Please. And take it with you.

DOROTHY   Oh, thank you so much! Now we can go back to the Wizard and tell him the Wicked Witch is dead!

WINKIES The Wicked Witch is dead!*

LAP DISSOLVE TO:
LONG SHOT—INT. THRONE ROOM

The atmosphere is the same as the first time they came before OZ.

DOROTHY, SCARECROW, LION, and TIN MAN are facing the throne. The great head is facing them from the throne.

OZ'S VOICE *(as shot opens)* Can I believe my eyes? Why have you come back?

DOROTHY *(on being handed broomstick by the SCARECROW)* Please, sir, we've done what you told us: we've brought you the broomstick of the Wicked Witch of the West.
(She puts the broomstick down at the foot of the throne.)
We melted her.

OZ'S VOICE Oh, you liquidated her, eh? Very resourceful.

DOROTHY Yes, sir. So we'd like you to keep your promise to us; if you please, sir.

OZ'S VOICE Not so fast! Not so fast! I'll have to give the matter a little thought! Go away and come back tomorrow!

DOROTHY Tomorrow? Oh, but I want to go home *now*!

TIN MAN You've had plenty of time already!

LION *(aggressively)* Yeah!

OZ'S VOICE *(roaring)* Do not arouse the wrath of the Great and Powerful Oz!

CAMERA PANS as TOTO runs to background to curtain hanging around side of throne room.

OZ'S VOICE *(cont'd.)* I said come back tomorrow!

DOROTHY If you were really great and powerful, you'd keep your promises!

* See Appendix D: The Triumphant Procession, pp. 142–143.

OZ'S VOICE   Do you presume to criticize the Great Oz?

TOTO pulls the curtain aside, and the WIZARD is revealed with his back to them talking into a microphone.

OZ'S VOICE   You ungrateful creatures!

They stare at the man working the controls of the throne.

OZ'S VOICE *(cont'd.)*   Think yourselves lucky that I'm giving you audience tomorrow instead of twenty years from now!
(A feeling that all is not as it should be makes the man look over his shoulder.)

WIZARD   Oh!

OZ'S VOICE   The Great Oz has spoken!

WIZARD   Oh!
(He pulls the curtain back.)

OZ'S VOICE   Pay no attention to that man behind the curtain! The Great Oz has spoken!

DOROTHY walks up quietly and pulls the curtain aside.

DOROTHY   Who are you?

WIZARD   Who are . . . ah . . . I am the Great and Powerful . . . Wizard of Oz.

DOROTHY *(unable to believe her ears)*   *You* are?

WIZARD   Uh—yes—

DOROTHY   I don't believe you!*

---

* The shooting script includes a gratuitous but still amusing scene not in the final film, that helped establish the Wizard as no more than a humbug:

WIZARD *(pulling out his handkerchief nervously)*   I fear so; yes.

SCARECROW *(angrily)*   I don't believe you! We've *seen* the Wizard—over there in smoke! You're just trying to stop us seeing him!

WIZARD *(turning the handkerchief into the flags of all nations)*   No, *really* I'm not! *(with a pathetic desire to please them)* Flags of all nations.

TIN MAN *(fiercely)*   Shall I chop his silly head off?

SCARECROW and LION   Yes!!

WIZARD   No, I'm afraid it's true. There's no other Wizard except me.

SCARECROW *(indignantly)*   You humbug!

LION and TIN MAN   Yeah!

WIZARD   Yes, that's exactly so. I'm a humbug.

DOROTHY   Oh, you're a very bad man!

WIZARD   Oh, no, my dear, I—I'm a very good man—I'm just a very bad wizard.

SCARECROW *(angrily)*   What about the heart that you promised Tin Man?

WIZARD   Well, I—

SCARECROW   And the courage that you promised Cowardly Lion?

WIZARD   Well, I—

TIN MAN and LION   And Scarecrow's brain?*

WIZARD *(in terror, rolling up the flags of all nations)*   No, no, please don't—I'll do anything you say, only please don't kill me! *(He turns the flags into a bunch of flowers. Still trying to impress them, in a wavering voice)* Bunch of flowers.

SCARECROW   Take us to the Wizard!

LION   Yeah, before I bite you!

WIZARD *(rolling up the flowers into a deck of cards)*   But, gentlemen, there *is* no Wizard except me! I'm *him,* truly I am . . .

Unfortunately Dorothy's friends as portrayed here are out of character, so the scene was wisely deleted.

* Deleted from the film was the following dialogue in the shooting script, paraphrasing Baum's book:

WIZARD   Well, I— But you've got them. You've had them all the time.

TIN MAN, LION, SCARECROW   Oh, no we haven't!

TIN MAN   You don't get out of it *that* way!

LION   Not nohow!

WIZARD   Well—

SCARECROW   You promised us *real things*—a real brain!

TIN MAN   A real heart!

LION   Real courage! That's what we want!

WIZARD   You do?

WIZARD *(to* SCARECROW*)*   Why, anybody can have a brain. That's a very mediocre commodity. Every pusillanimous creature that crawls on the earth or slinks through slimy seas has a brain! Back where I come from, we have universities, seats of great learning—where men go to become great thinkers, and when they come out, they think deep thoughts—and with no more brains than you have —*but!* they have one thing you haven't got! A diploma.
(He picks up several diplomas, selects a parchment scroll with seal and ribbon, and presents it to the SCARECROW.*)*
Therefore—by virtue of the authority vested in me by the *Universitatus Committeeatum e pluribus unum,* I hereby confer upon you the honorary degree of Th.D. Heh, heh!

SCARECROW *(terribly impressed)*   Th.D.?

WIZARD   Yeah, that . . . that's Doctor of Thinkology.

SCARECROW *(putting his finger to his head)*   The sum of the square roots of any two sides of an isosceles triangle is equal to the square root of the remaining side. Oh, joy, rapture! I've got a brain! How can I ever thank you enough?

WIZARD   Well, you can't. *(turning to* LION*)* As for you, my fine friend, you're a victim of disorganized thinking. You are under the unfortunate delusion that simply because you run away from danger, you have no courage. You're confusing courage with wisdom. Back where I come from, we have men who are called heroes. Once a year they take their fortitude out of mothballs and parade it down the main street of the city. And they have no more courage than you have—*but!* they have one thing that you haven't got! A medal!
(He takes a big triple-cross medal out of his black bag and pins it on the LION*'s skin as he imitates a French Legion general.)*
Therefore, for meritorious conduct, extraordinary valor, conspicuous bravery against wicked witches, I award you the Triple Cross. You are now a member of the Legion of Courage.
(He kisses LION *on both cheeks.)*

(derogatory)
Boys, you're aiming low. You not only surprise, but grieve me. . . .

LION *(overcome)* Hah, hah, shucks, folks, I'm speechless! Hah, hah . . . *(hides his face)*

WIZARD *(to* TIN MAN*)* As for you, my galvanized friend, you want a heart! You don't know how lucky you are not to have one. Hearts will never be practical until they can be made unbreakable.

TIN MAN But I . . . I still want one.

WIZARD Back where I come from, there are men who do nothing all day but good deeds. They are called phil . . . er . . . phil . . . er . . . yes . . . er . . . good-deed-doers, and their hearts are no bigger than yours—*but!* they have one thing you haven't got! A testimonial!
(He takes a huge heart-shaped watch and chain out of his black bag.)
Therefore, in consideration of your kindness, I take pleasure at this time in presenting you with a small token of our esteem and affection. *(hands it to* TIN MAN*)* And remember, my sentimental friend, that a heart is not judged by how much you love, but by how much you are loved by others.

TIN MAN *(listening to the watch, in ecstasy, sighs)* Ah, eh, oh, it ticks! *(showing it to* DOROTHY*)*

DOROTHY Oh, yes!

TIN MAN Listen! Look, it ticks!

LION *(to* DOROTHY*)* Read . . . read what my medal says! "Courage!" Ain't it the truth! Ain't it the truth!

DOROTHY *(joyfully)* Oh . . . oh, they're all wonderful . . .

SCARECROW *(suddenly—to* WIZARD*)* Hey, what about Dorothy?

TIN MAN Yes, how about Dorothy?

LION Yeah.

WIZARD Ah . . .

LION Dorothy next!

WIZARD Yes, Dorothy . . . ah . . .

DOROTHY *(sadly)* Oh, I don't think there's anything in that black bag for me.

WIZARD Well, you force me into a cataclysmic decision. The only way to get Dorothy back to Kansas is for me to take her there myself.

DOROTHY *(her face lighting up)* Oh, will you? Could you? Oh! *(with doubt)* Oh, but are you a clever enough wizard to manage it?

WIZARD *(with dignity)* Child, you cut me to the quick! I'm an old Kansas man myself . . . born and bred in the heart of the Western wilderness, premier balloonist par excellence to the Miracle Wonderland Carnival Company—until one day, while performing spectacular feats of stratospheric skill never before attempted by civilized man, an unfortunate phenomena occurred. The balloon failed to return to the fair.

LION It *did?*

DOROTHY Weren't you frightened?

WIZARD *(leading them toward the door)* Frightened! You are talking to a man who has laughed in the face of death, sneered at doom, and chuckled at catastrophe. I was petrified! Then suddenly the wind changed, and the balloon floated down into the heart of this noble city, where I was instantly acclaimed Oz, the First Wizard de luxe! *(laughs)*

DOROTHY Oh!

WIZARD Times being what they were, I accepted the job, heh, retaining my balloon against the advent of a quick getaway. Ha ha! And in that balloon, my dear Dorothy, you and I will return to the land of *e pluribus unum!* Ha ha! And now . . .

They all laugh and begin walking out of the room, CAMERA TRUCKING with them.

LAP DISSOLVE:
LONG SHOT—EMERALD CITY SQUARE

On a decorated platform erected in the center of the square and surrounded by the people of Oz stands the gaily striped balloon with DOROTHY and the WIZARD in it. The SCARECROW, TIN MAN, and LION stand near, in charge of the mooring ropes. The balloon reads: STATE FAIR OMAHA. The square is filled with cheering people.

WIZARD *(as shot opens)*   My friends, my friends, I mean *my friends*! . . . This is positively the finest exhibition ever to be shown . . . well . . . eh . . . well . . . be that as it may—I, your Wizard *par ardua ad alta,* am about to embark upon a hazardous and technically unexplainable journey into the outer stratosphere . . .
(Crowd cheers.)
. . . to confer, converse, and otherwise hobnob with my brother wizards, and I hereby decree that until what time—
(aside)
—if any—
(aloud)
—that I return, the Scarecrow by virtue of his highly superior brains, shall rule in my stead, assisted by the Tin Man, by virtue of his magnificent heart, and the Lion, by virtue of his courage! Obey them as you would me! Thank you!

CLOSEUP—TOTO IN DOROTHY'S ARMS

He suddenly cocks his ears and growls.

CLOSE SHOT—OZ WOMAN WITH CAT IN HER ARMS

The CAT meows.

MEDIUM SHOT—DOROTHY IN BALLOON BASKET

TOTO jumps out of her arms.

DOROTHY   Oh, Toto! Come back! Toto! Toto!
(She jumps out of basket.)
Oh, don't go without me! I'll be right with you! Toto!
(She runs down steps.)

LONG SHOT—BALLOON BASKET

TIN MAN   Stop that dog!

DOROTHY Toto!

The SCARECROW and the LION drop the ropes to help DORO-THY. The balloon begins to rise.

WIZARD This is a highly irregular procedure! . . . absolutely unprecedented!

TIN MAN Oh, help me! The balloon's going up!

WIZARD . . . Ruined my exit!

DOROTHY and SCARECROW return to platform as the balloon rises.

DOROTHY *(in a scream)* Oh! Come back, come back—don't go without me! Please come back!

WIZARD I can't come back! I don't know how it works!
(waving to the crowd)
Good-bye, folks!

PEOPLE *(waving back)* Good-bye! Good-bye! Good-bye! Good-bye!

The balloon passes over the cheering crowd and out of sight.

MEDIUM SHOT—DOROTHY AND TOTO

as the SCARECROW, TIN MAN, and LION try to comfort her.

DOROTHY *(in terrible distress)* Oh, now I'll *never* get home!

LION Stay with us, then, Dorothy. We all love ya. We don't want ya to go.

DOROTHY Oh, that's very kind of you, but this could never be like Kansas. Auntie Em must have stopped wondering what happened to me by now. Oh, Scarecrow, what am I going to do?

SCARECROW *(pointing)* Look! Here's someone who can help you!

LONG SHOT—EMERALD CITY SQUARE

The WITCH OF THE NORTH'S BUBBLE floats over the crowd. The people step aside as it comes to rest and fades. GLINDA approaches, waving her wand.

PEOPLE Oh . . . my . . .

DOROTHY *(curtsying)* Oh, *will* you help me? *Can* you help me?

GLINDA You don't need to be helped any longer. You've always had the power to go back to Kansas.

DOROTHY I *have?*

SCARECROW Then why didn't you tell her before?

GLINDA Because she wouldn't have believed me. She had to learn it for herself.

SCARECROW and TIN MAN look inquiringly at DOROTHY.

TIN MAN What have you learned, Dorothy?

DOROTHY *(thoughtfully)* Well, I . . . I think that it . . . that it wasn't enough just to want to see Uncle Henry and Auntie Em . . . and it's that if I ever go looking for my heart's desire again, I won't look any further than my own backyard; because if it isn't there, I never really lost it to begin with!
(timidly to GLINDA)
Is that right?

GLINDA *(nodding and smiling)* That's all it is.

SCARECROW But that's so easy! I should have thought of it *for* you!

TIN MAN I should have felt it in my heart!

GLINDA No—she had to find it out for herself. Now those magic slippers will take you home in two seconds!

DOROTHY Oh! Toto, too?

GLINDA Toto, too.

DOROTHY *(overjoyed)* Oh, now?

GLINDA Whenever you wish.

DOROTHY turns delightedly to the others.

DOROTHY Oh, dear, that's too wonderful to be true!
(in a small voice, her eyes in tears)

Oh, it's . . . it's going to be so hard to say good-bye. I love *you* all, too. Good-bye, Tin Man. Oh, don't cry . . .
(wiping away his tears) (handing him his oil can)
. . . You'll rust so dreadfully. Here . . . here's your oil can.
(She kisses him.)
Good-bye.

TIN MAN   Now I know I've got a heart . . . 'Cause it's breaking.

DOROTHY *(to* LION, *kissing him)*   Good-bye, Lion. You know, I know it isn't right, but I'm going to miss the way you used to holler for help before you found your courage!

LION   I—I would never've found it if it hadn't been for you.

DOROTHY turns to SCARECROW; they look at each other a second, then she puts her arms around him and hugs him.

DOROTHY *(whispering in* SCARECROW'*s ear)*   I think I'll miss you most of all. *(She kisses him and sobs.)*

GLINDA   Are you ready now?

DOROTHY   Yes. Say good-bye, Toto.
(She waves TOTO'*s paw at her friends; they wave in return.)*
Yes, I'm ready now.

GLINDA   Then close your eyes and tap your heels together three times . . .

CLOSEUP—RUBY SLIPPERS

DOROTHY clicks them together three times.

GLINDA *(cont'd.)*   . . . and think to yourself, "There's no place like home; there's no place like home; there's no . . ."

CAMERA TRUCKS FORWARD to DOROTHY as she speaks with her eyes closed.

DOROTHY   ". . . there's no place like home; there's no place like home . . ."

DOROTHY's face remains in BIG CLOSEUP while superimposed

with spiral effect and then CLOSEUP of RUBY SLIPPERS clicking together three times.

DOROTHY ". . . there's no place like home; there's no place like home; there's no place like home . . ."*

LONG SHOT—DOROTHY'S HOUSE

falling toward CAMERA with a crash to BLACKOUT.

(SEPIA TONE)
FADE IN—CLOSEUP—DOROTHY—INT. DOROTHY'S BED-ROOM

We are on DOROTHY's face, with eyes closed, as she is murmuring:

DOROTHY ". . . there's no place like home; there's no place like home; there's no place like home . . ."

A wet cloth is being applied to her forehead.

AUNT EM Wake up, honey.

At this DOROTHY opens her eyes and looks up.

DOROTHY ". . . there's no place like home; there's no place like home . . . there's no place . . ."

CAMERA TRUCKS BACK to see AUNT EM sitting on Dorothy's bed. UNCLE HENRY is standing, looking down at her anxiously.

AUNT EM Dorothy—Dorothy, dear . . . It's Aunt Em, darling.

DOROTHY *(with happy excitement)* Oh, Auntie Em, it's *you* . . .

AUNT EM *(removing the cloth)* Yes, darling.

From offscreen we hear the PROFESSOR's voice calling:

PROFESSOR MARVEL Hello, there! Anybody home?

---

* The original montage filmed for Dorothy's return to Kansas was entirely different from that in the final picture: The Munchkins waving good-bye from the border of Munchkinland; the Witch laughing; the Wizard at his control panel in the throne room turning and pulling the curtain; Glinda leading the Munchkins in a dance; the Lion growling; the Tin Man breaking in the door of the Witch's tower room; Hickory's wind machine on the Gale farm; horses looking out from stalls; chickens moving about; and Aunt Em offering a plate of crullers.

(He passes by window and stops.) I . . . I just dropped by because I heard the little girl got caught in the big—
(smiling at DOROTHY *as he sees her)*
Well, she seems all right now.

UNCLE HENRY   Yeah, she got quite a bump on the head. We kinda thought there for a minute she was gonna leave us.

PROFESSOR MARVEL   Oh.

DOROTHY   But I *did* leave you, Uncle Henry—that's just the trouble! And I tried to get back for days and days—

AUNT EM *(soothingly)*   There, there, lie quiet now. You just had a bad dream—

DOROTHY   No . . .

HUNK, HICKORY, and ZEKE approach the bed.

HUNK   Sure—remember me? Your old pal, Hunk?

DOROTHY   Oh—

HICKORY   Me, Hickory?

ZEKE   You couldn't forget my face, could ya?

DOROTHY   No, but it wasn't a dream. It was a place.
(as she points to the THREE BOYS*)*
And you—and you—and you—
(points to the PROFESSOR*)*
And *you* were there!

PROFESSOR MARVEL   Oh!

HUNK   Sure.

They all laugh.

DOROTHY *(puzzled)*   But you couldn't have been, could you?

AUNT EM *(gently)*   Oh, we dream lots of silly things when we—

DOROTHY *(with absolute belief)*   No, Aunt Em, this was a real truly live place. And I remember that some of it wasn't very nice—but most of it was beautiful! But just the same, all I kept saying to everybody was, "I want to go home." And they sent me home! *(She waits for a reaction; they all laugh again.)* Doesn't anybody believe me?

UNCLE HENRY *(soberly, softly)* Of course we believe you, Dorothy . . .

TOTO crawls on the bed to DOROTHY.

DOROTHY Oh, but anyway, Toto, we're home—*home!* And this is my room—and you're all here—and I'm not going to leave here ever, ever again, because I love you all! And . . . oh, Auntie Em, there's no place like home!

FADE OUT:
FADE IN:
The End

FADE OUT:

FADE IN:

CAST

Dorothy . . . . *JUDY GARLAND*
Professor Marvel . . . . *FRANK MORGAN*
"Hunk" . . . . *RAY BOLGER*
"Zeke" . . . . *BERT LAHR*
"Hickory" . . . . *JACK HALEY*
Glinda . . . . *BILLIE BURKE*
Miss Gulch . . . . *MARGARET HAMILTON*
Uncle Henry . . . . *CHARLEY GRAPEWIN*
Nikko . . . . *PAT WALSHE*
Auntie Em . . . . *CLARA BLANDICK*
Toto . . . . *TOTO*
The Singer Midgets As The Munchkins

FADE OUT

APPENDICES:
DELETED SCENES AND
ADDITIONAL LYRICS

APPENDIX A
THE SCARECROW'S DANCE

CLOSE SHOT—SCARECROW

seated on the road. CAMERA PULLS back as he feels about his coat. DOROTHY points to some of his straw on the road. A CROW flies in and lands near the straw. The SCARECROW trembles with fear. DOROTHY comforts him.

The CROW picks up the straw in his mouth and flies past them. CAMERA BOOMS up as the SCARECROW goes over to the fence and shakes his fist at the CROW flying over the cornfield.

The SCARECROW dances back along the road. DOROTHY rushes to him and stops him and points to the CROW landing in the field.

He reassures her. CAMERA PULLS back as he dances forward, begins to run, and makes a big jump, landing in a cornfield. Several CROWS fly out of the corn.

DOROTHY runs over to the fence. The SCARECROW moves through the cornstalks. He bends down, finds his straw, and stuffs it back into his coat. He runs forward, jumps in the air, and soars over the field. DOROTHY waves to him.

The SCARECROW falls to the Yellow Brick Road. CAMERA PULLS back as DOROTHY rushes to him. The SCARECROW begins to dance again, doing a series of splits.

TOTO jumps on a pumpkin and starts it rolling along the Yellow Brick Road. It hits the SCARECROW, knocking him high into the air. DOROTHY looks on, frightened.

CAMERA PANS up with the SCARECROW as he soars into the air. DOROTHY watches him. He falls back onto the Yellow Brick Road. He runs off.

CAMERA PULLS back as the SCARECROW dances forward, bumping into one side of the fence, then bouncing from that to the fence on the other side of the road, then back to the fence on the left, and so on down the road. CAMERA PANS right with him as he runs past DOROTHY and falls through a fence, which breaks under his weight. The SCARECROW sits up, looks about, and blinks his eyes.

DOROTHY watches. REVERSE ACTION shot of the SCARE-CROW bouncing from fence to fence along the road. He starts to dance back.

SCARECROW *(singing)*
Gosh, it would be awful pleasin'
To reason out a reason
For things I can't explain
Then perhaps I'll deserve you
And be even worthy erv you
If I only had a brain.

Some more straw has fallen out. He slumps down to the road. DOR-OTHY starts to bend down.

APPENDIX B
THE BEEHIVE

TIN MAN *(heartily)* I'll see you reach the Wizard, whether I get a heart or not. Beehive—bah! Let her try and make a beehive out of me! *(snaps his fingers)* You know—Hmm? What's that?

Suddenly there is a faint buzz from inside the TIN MAN. A look of disbelief comes into his face, and he thumps himself on the chest. The buzzing increases; he begins to wriggle and writhe and cough and sputter; the buzzing increases; he opens his mouth. First one, then two bees fly out. DOROTHY and the SCARECROW scramble for cover.

TRICK SHOT—TIN MAN

This shot is tricked so that a whole swarm of bees pour out of the TIN MAN's mouth, ears, and the tin funnel in his hat.

TIN MAN Oh! They're—they're gone now.

DOROTHY Oh, goodness! Did any of them sting you?

TIN MAN I—I guess they tried to, but they bent their stingers.

DOROTHY Oh, dear. I don't know what I'd do if a whole swarm kept—*(sees bee on her arm)* Oh! Oh! Oh, there's one on me!

TIN MAN Oh—I'll get it! *(takes bee off her arm)*

DOROTHY Oh! Oh! Oh!

TIN MAN *(cries)* Oh, see—I killed it. Oh, I killed that poor little honeybee!

DOROTHY Oh-oh—

TIN MAN *(still crying)* It's only a man without a heart who could do a thing like that. Poor little bee.

DOROTHY Oh, there . . . *(wipes away his tears)* . . . there. Don't cry. There. As a matter of fact, that's just an old drone bee, and it would have died anyway.

TIN MAN Yes?

DOROTHY You put it out of its misery.

TIN MAN   Oh.

DOROTHY *(in great distress)*   It's just that the Witch is so wicked. I don't think you two ought to come with me, because you'll get into trouble.

SCARECROW *(indignantly)*   Oh, you don't think we're going to stand by and let her get away with fireballs and bees, do you?

TIN MAN *(valiantly)*   No, sir!

SCARECROW   No, sir!

They all laugh.

APPENDIX C
THE JITTERBUG

HAUNTED FOREST—LONG SHOT—FOUR

SHOOTING from behind them as they advance cautiously, step by step. The whine of the jitterbug comes in on TRACK.

CLOSE ON LION'S NOSE

A large pink and blue spotted MOSQUITO lands on his nose. He jumps round, slapping it with his paw.

LION *(fearfully)* What's that? What's that? Take it away—take it away—take it away! *(cries)*

TIN MAN Hold still—hold still—

LONG SHOT—THREE

DOROTHY suddenly jumps and slaps her ankle.

DOROTHY Oh! Something bit me, too!

TIN MAN Now, come on. You're acting silly— Ouch!

SCARECROW Oh, come on now. Everybody— Ouch!

The music grows spookier and spookier.

FULL SHOT—TREES ALL ABOUT

All the branches and leaves are quivering in rhythm. This number is sung as they "jitter" and shiver their way along the path.

DOROTHY *Did you hear what I just heard?*

LION *That noise don't come from no ordinary bird.*

DOROTHY
*It may be just a cricket
Or a critter in the trees.*

TIN MAN
*It's giving me the jitters
In the joints around my knees.*

SCARECROW
Oh, I think I see a jijik

And he's fuzzy and he's furry
I haven't got a brain
But I think I ought to worry.

TIN MAN
I haven't got a heart
But I got a palpitation.

LION
As Monarch of the Forest
I don't like the situation.

DOROTHY *(to* LION*)*
Are you gonna stand around
And let 'em fill us full of horror?

LION
I'd like to roar 'em down . . .
But I think I lost my roarer.

LONG SHOT—FOUR

running around as the trees shiver. They huddle together.

TIN MAN   It's a whozis.

SCARECROW   It's a whozis?

LION   It's a whatzis.

TIN MAN   It's a whatzis?

LION   Whozat?

TIN MAN   Whozat?

SCARECROW   Whozat?

DOROTHY   Whozat?
(singing chorus)
Who's that hiding
In the tree top?
It's that rascal
The Jitterbug.

Should you catch him
Buzzin' 'round you
Keep away from
The Jitterbug!

They all dance.

DOROTHY *(cont'd.)*
Oh, the bats and the bees
And the breeze in the trees
Have a terrible, horrible buzz
But the bats and the bees
And the breeze in the trees
Couldn't do what the Jitterbug does.

So be careful
Of that rascal
Keep away from—

SCARECROW, TIN MAN, and LION
—The Jitterbug!
Oh, the Jitter
Oh, the Bug
Oh, the Jitter—

ALL   *Bug-bug-a-bug-bug-bug-bug-bug-a-boo!*

The LION runs over to a TREE, which catches hold of his tail. The SCARECROW runs over and is caught when the TREE releases the LION. He struggles free. CAMERA PANS as he runs over to DOROTHY, who is held by another TREE. The TIN MAN starts to chop the TREE down, and a limb of the TREE hits him over the head, staggering him as he throws his ax away.

ALL *(dancing)*
In a twitter
In the throes

SCARECROW
Oh, the critter's got me dancin'
On a thousand toes.

TIN MAN
Thar' she blows!

They all continue dancing as the TREES move in rhythm.

LONG SHOT—WINGED MONKEYS

flying over the Haunted Forest.

LONG SHOT—FOUR

stop dancing and look up.

APPENDIX D
THE TRIUMPHANT PROCESSION

DOROTHY   Oh, thank you so much! Now we can go back to the Wizard and tell him the Wicked Witch is dead!

LEADER OF THE WINKIES   The Wicked Witch is dead!

ALL *(forming an arc with their spears)*
The Wicked Witch is dead! The Wicked Witch is dead!
(singing)*
Hail—Hail—the witch is dead!
Which old witch? The wicked witch!
Hail—Hail—the wicked witch is dead!
Hail—Hail—the witch is dead!
Which old witch? The wicked witch . . .

LAP DISSOLVE TO:
LONG SHOT—THE EMERALD CITY

Streets are thronged with cheering people as a procession passes by led by a marching band.

ALL *(singing)*
Hail—Hail—the wicked witch is dead!
Ding Dong, the witch is dead!
Which old witch? The wicked witch!
Ding Dong, the wicked witch is dead!

As the procession comes forward through the crowded streets, DOROTHY, the TIN MAN, the LION, and the SCARECROW are surrounded by FLOWER GIRLS. The SCARECROW is carrying the Witch's broomstick.

ALL *(singing)*
Wake up, you sleepy head,
Rub your eyes,
Get out of bed.
Wake up, the wicked witch is dead!
She's gone where the goblins go

* Aljean Harmetz reports in *The Making of The Wizard of Oz* (p. 83) that Yip Harburg suggested an alternative lyric to be sung by the Winkies and Winged Monkeys:
Ding Dong! She met her fate
We liqui-dated her!

Below, below, below,
Yo ho let's open up and sing,
And ring the bells out:
Ding Dong! the merry-o
Sing it high,
Sing it low,
Let them know
The wicked witch is dead!
Ding Dong, The witch is dead!
Which old witch? The wicked witch!
Ding Dong, the wicked witch is dead!

CAMERA PANS right with the PROCESSION as it marches toward the Palace. CAMERA BOOMS around to one of the huge
crystals as the TIN MAN, DOROTHY, SCARECROW, and LION
enter through the Palace gates.

ALL (singing)
Wake up, you sleepy head,
Rub your eyes,
Get out of bed.
Wake up, the wicked witch is dead!
She's gone where the goblins go
Below, below, below,
Yo ho let's open up and sing,
And ring the bells out:
Ding Dong! the merry-o
Sing it high . . .

APPENDIX E
THE RAINBOW BRIDGE

WITCH'S VOICE *(mimicking)*   Aunt Em—Aunt Em—come back! I'll give you Aunt Em, my pretty!

The WITCH's clawlike HAND comes into the SHOT from the outside and clutches DOROTHY's shoulder. DRAW CAMERA BACK to show that the face in the crystal is a reflection of the real WITCH, who has come back into the room and is standing behind DOROTHY.

As DOROTHY shrinks back with a muffled exclamation of terror, the WITCH pulls her to her feet.

WITCH *(with an evil smile)*   I have a little work for you to do.

FOLLOW WITH CAMERA as she pushes DOROTHY toward the door, which is held open by NIKKO.

WITCH *(cont'd.)*   It's bad for girls to be idle—very, very bad.

As DOROTHY comes through the door, she shrinks back at the sight of four WINKIE GUARDS, who are standing in the hall beyond. The WINKIES are huge figures with grotesque and hideous headdresses like the death's-head helmets in Japanese armor. They are absolutely inhuman.

WITCH *(to DOROTHY)*   Take that pail and mop! *(as DOROTHY obeys)* You are to scrub every floor in this castle—do you hear? Every floor! *(she adds, with an evil smile)* Because by tomorrow you may not be here to scrub anymore.

She signals to the WINKIE GUARDS. As they close in on the frightened girl,

LAP DISSOLVE TO:

[TOTO goes in search of the SCARECROW, TIN MAN, and COWARDLY LION—as in film.]

FADE IN ON:
A ROOM IN THE WITCH'S CASTLE

Some hours have presumably passed, and Dorothy is wearily mopping a hallway.

NOTE: *This room should be built with an eye to perspective so that we look down what seems to be an endless corridor with huge and ominous WINKIE GUARDS stationed at intervals and the tiny little figure of DOROTHY in the foreground.*

DOROTHY looks tired and exhausted, but every time she tries to stop and rest, one of the WINKIES points with his spear toward another spot in the floor, and she is forced to start on again.

FOLLOW HER WITH CAMERA as she goes over to a fountain, which is on a little open court high up on the side of the castle (like the little wall-terrace fountains in an Italian villa) to refill her bucket. She pauses for a moment, leaning out looking at the view, which includes a beautiful full moon to one side of the castle. Suddenly she sees something far below.

LONG SHOT—FROM DOROTHY'S ANGLE

Far away down the mountainside THREE little figures are being led upward by a DOG. We catch just a glimpse of them as they pass between the trees.

CLOSEUP—DOROTHY

as she sees this and realizes help is on its way. Her whole face flashes into a smile. She bends over to call, then suddenly glances back over her shoulder toward the GUARDS in the hall behind her. She realizes they would be sure to hear her. Suddenly she has an idea. As she fills her bucket at the fountain, she begins to sing, "Over the Rainbow."

CLOSE ON DOROTHY

as she sings, putting all her heart and soul into her song. What was a happy song in Kansas becomes infinitely pathetic now. We, the audience, should realize that the lovely land over the rainbow for which she yearns is no longer a foreign land, but Kansas—the farm—
home.

HILLSIDE

where the COWARDLY LION is fighting his way over the boulders and slippery shale, with the TIN MAN holding on to his tail. The

SCARECROW is pushing the TIN MAN up from behind. They are being led by TOTO.

Dorothy's SONG is coming very faintly on the SOUNDTRACK, but as they come around a big boulder, it grows louder.

They all turn and look up.

SCARECROW and TIN MAN *(together)* Listen! It's Dorothy! She's up there!

LONG SHOT—WITCH'S CASTLE FROM THEIR ANGLE

This is a miniature showing the great pointed towers of the castle silhouetted against the sky on the peak of the mountain. The SONG still comes over the SOUNDTRACK. There is a full moon, which makes it almost as bright as day.

BACK TO:
SCENE

as they start up with renewed energy. The TIN MAN takes hold of the LION's tail, the SCARECROW pushes him, and the THREE start off again after TOTO.

CUT BACK TO:
DOROTHY

still singing.

CUT TO:
INT. WITCH'S TOWER ROOM

The window is closed, so that Dorothy's SONG is heard faintly. The beldame is talking angrily to NIKKO.

WITCH Mocking me by singing, eh?

She pushes the window open furiously, just in time to get the end of the SONG: "Birds fly over the rainbow—why then, oh why can't I?" A cruel smile lights her face.

WITCH *(cont'd.)* So she wants to go over the rainbow, does she?

SWING THE CAMERA WITH HER as she hobbles, clucking back to a dark corner, with NIKKO following. Here she opens a huge iron-bound chest, which is covered with dust and cobwebs.

WITCH *(cont'd.)* So long as that girl is alive, I'll never get those slippers—but I have a little idea . . .

She takes out a parchment scroll. NIKKO holds a candle while she unrolls it.

INSERT—CLOSE ON PARCHMENT

It is stained with age. In ancient, illuminated script we read, "Spells for Making Rain . . . Raindrops . . . Rainbows." As her finger follows these, the WITCH'S VOICE reads some rhymed couplets.

NOTE: *Mr. Harburg is working these rhymes out for us.*

As she mumbles the directions for making a rainbow,

CUT TO:

[The SCARECROW, TIN MAN, and COWARDLY LION enter the Witch's castle, disguised as three WINKIE GUARDS—as in film.]

HALLWAY AT TOP OF STAIRS

This outside the door to the Witch's room. The THREE COMRADES are just coming up to the door. They pause and listen. Someone is humming "Over the Rainbow" inside.

SCARECROW *(whispering)* Dorothy must be in there.

The others nod. MOVE CAMERA with them as they open the door and start to tiptoe into the room.

LONGER ON SCENE

This shows the WITCH is busy at her caldron. She is humming the rainbow song as she brews her spell, stirring now and again, and the scroll is open beside her.

CLOSER ON THREE

as they discover they have walked in on the WITCH instead of DOROTHY. For a moment they are frightened, then the TIN MAN takes a firmer grip on his ax, the SCARECROW on his spanner, and the LION forces himself to bravery. MOVE CAMERA with them as they creep up behind her back.

CLOSE ON WITCH

as she looks into her caldron, which is boiling merrily. All the brilliant colors found in a prism are reflected upward into her face from the bubbling mass.

WITCH *(delightedly, to* NIKKO, *who stands beside her)* Aha—ready! And just in time!

As she walks, we see the SCARECROW, LION, and TIN MAN close behind her. They raise their arms with the ax and spanner. For one moment it looks as if they are going to succeed in polishing off the old horror.

LONGER ON SCENE

to show that three WINKIES have come out of the shadows and are standing close behind them. The WITCH, still stirring, gives a cackling laugh.

WITCH Good evening, my friends.
(She swings around and grins at them evilly as the WINKIES *seize them from behind.)*
I've been expecting you for some time.

SCARECROW, TIN MAN, and LION *(all together, as they struggle in the grasp of the* WINKIES*)* You let us go! Where's Dorothy? What have you done with her?

WITCH *(laughing)* Dorothy? Dorothy? Why, I haven't done anything to Dorothy. I've been waiting for the moon.
(as she moves toward the window and looks out)
Ah—it's just right—directly over the castle.
(She turns back to them.)
I'm going to let *you* destroy her.

SCARECROW, TIN MAN We won't! You can't make us!

WITCH You won't be able to help yourselves. Look!

(She waves her broomstick toward the caldron.)

CLOSER ON CALDRON

as the colors begin to boil and reflect over the walls behind the fire.

CLOSER BY WINDOW

The WITCH makes a sweeping movement with her broomstick. The others shrink back.

WITCH *(cont'd.) (shrilly)*   I'll give you a rainbow, my pretty dear. I'll give you a *moon*bow!

CLOSER ON WINDOW

This is looking out through the highly arched window. Flashes of glorious, blinding color start swirling. They are reflected against a far tower on the other side of the courtyard.

LONG SHOT—CASTLE—MINIATURE—TRICK SHOT

A rainbow has formed a bridge between the two towers. This is very long and passes across the whole courtyard, which is a great distance below. It is a beautiful sight, but, like all rainbows, it grows thinner and thinner as it curves upward. The general effect is like one of the lovely curved bridges in Venice.

INT. WITCH'S TOWER ROOM

as the SCARECROW, TIN MAN, and LION look out and see the rainbow curving up from outside the big window.

WITCH *(cont'd.) (gloatingly)*   Ha! My old hand hasn't lost its cunning! Now to try it out!
(She claps her hands. The most hideous of the WINKIE GUARDS comes in. She speaks to him.)
Dorothy is across there in that tower room. Bring her to me.
(sharply, as he salutes and turns back toward the door)
Not that way, fool! Use the new bridge.

Without any change of expression, the WINKIE goes to the window.

LONG SHOT—BRIDGE

as the GUARD marches up, with his eyes straight ahead in a military fashion. He reaches the center of the bridge.

CLOSE ON GUARD

as he realizes he is falling through. An expression of mingled surprise and horror comes over his hideous countenance. He clutches for support, but there is nothing to hold him.

LONGER SHOT

as he falls through the center of the rainbow.

INT. WITCH'S TOWER ROOM

The WITCH is looking down into the courtyard with an expression of fiendish delight.

WITCH *(cont'd.)*   It works! It works!
(She grins at the horrified SCARECROW*)*
Now you will call Dorothy over.

SCARECROW   No—no—I won't! You can't make me!
(The WITCH *points her broomstick at him. He chokes, struggles to finish his words.)*
I w-won't . . .
(in spite of himself, he calls)
Dorothy—Dorothy!

The WITCH points the broomstick at the TIN MAN, who goes through the same agonized struggle, but ends by calling DORO-THY.

INT. TOWER ROOM—NOT THE WITCH'S

DOROTHY is standing, wearily against her mop. Suddenly she hears voices calling, looks surprised, runs up some stone steps, which lead to the top of the tower. The rainbow music is playing softly on the SOUNDTRACK with, possibly, the witch's theme in counter melody to give it menace.

LONGER SHOT—TOP OF TOWER

DOROTHY runs out, trying to find where the voices are coming from. She looks over, sees the beautiful rainbow bridge leading to the window of the Witch's tower room. All of her friends are visible beyond. With a glad cry, she starts up the side of the rainbow bridge, still carrying her pail and mop.

LONG SHOT—TRICK SHOT

showing the little figure running up the curve of the rainbow bridge.

INT. WITCH'S TOWER ROOM

as her FRIENDS realize DOROTHY's peril. They tear themselves away from the spell of the WITCH and lean out the window, screaming at her to go back.

CLOSE ON DOROTHY

who has almost reached the top of the curve. She sees her FRIENDS motioning her to go back. Suddenly she looks down.

LONG SHOT—FROM DOROTHY'S ANGLE PAST HER FEET

This shows the thinness of the rainbow, with the courtyard a great distance below.

CLOSE ON DOROTHY

as she realizes her peril. Her face expresses terror. For one moment she is appalled, then suddenly pulls herself together, throws back her head.

DOROTHY   I'm not afraid.

LONG SHOT—DOROTHY

as her little RUBY SLIPPERS seem to come to life with an iridescent glow. They run across the perilous center of the bridge as though carrying her with them.

INT. WITCH'S TOWER ROOM

as DOROTHY runs down the descending side of the bridge and falls into the arms of her FRIENDS.

WITCH (screaming and beating the floor with her broomstick)   It's those slippers! You couldn't have done it without those slippers!

APPENDIX F
ADDITIONAL LYRICS

When the songs of *The Wizard of Oz* were published by Leo Feist, Inc. in 1939, Yip Harburg and Harold Arlen revised the numbers to replace the dialogue that had introduced them in the motion picture and to set them up outside the context of the film.

1. *"Over the Rainbow"*:
   When all the world is a hopeless jumble
   And raindrops tumble
   All around,
   Heaven opens a magic lane.
   When all the clouds darken up the skyway,
   There's a rainbow highway
   To be found,
   Leading from your windowpane.
   To a place behind the sun,
   Just a step beyond the rain . . .

The British version includes a second verse which may *not* have been written by Harburg:

   Once by a word only lightly spoken
   All your dreams are broken
   For a while,
   Sadness comes and joy goes by;
   But ev'ry tear like the rain descending
   Finds a happy ending
   In a smile,
   Doubts and fears all fade and die
   To the blue beyond the grey
   Love again will find its way. . . .

2. *"Ding Dong! The Witch Is Dead"*:
   Once there was a wicked witch
   In the lovely land of Oz,
   And a wickeder, wickeder, wickeder witch
   There never, never was.
   She filled the folks in Munchkinland
   With terror and with dread,
   Till one fine day

From Kansas way
A cyclone caught
A house that brought
The wicked, wicked witch her doom
As she was flying on her broom.
For the house fell on her head
And the coroner pronounced her dead,
And through the town the joyous news was spread . . .

3. *"We're Off to See the Wizard (The Wonderful Wizard of Oz)":*
Follow the yellow brick road,
Follow the yellow brick road,
Follow, follow, follow, follow,
Follow the yellow brick road.
Follow the rainbow over the stream,
Follow the fellow who follows a dream,
Follow, follow, follow, follow,
Follow the yellow brick road. . . .

4. *"If I Only Had a Brain . . . a Heart . . . the Nerve":*
(SCARECROW) *Said a scarecrow swingin' on a pole*
To a blackbird sittin' on a fence,
"Oh! the Lord gave me a soul
But forgot to give me common sense.
If I had an ounce of sense . . ."
(TIN MAN) *Said a tin man rattlin' his gibs*
To a strawman sad and weary-eyed,
"Oh! the Lord gave me tin ribs
But forgot to put a heart inside."
Then he banged his hollow chest and cried . . .
(LION) *Said a lion, poor neurotic lion,*
To a miss who listened to him rave,
"Oh! the Lord made me a lion,
But the Lord forgot to make me brave."
Then his tail began to curl and wave.
Life is sad believe me missy
When you're born to be a sissy,
Without the vim and verve.
But I could change my habits,

Never more be scared of rabbits
If I only had the nerve.
I'm afraid there's no denyin'
I'm just a dandelion,
A fate I don't deserve.
But I could show my prowess,
Be a lion, not a mowess,
If I only had the nerve.
Oh, I'd be in my stride,
A king down to the core,
Oh I'd roar the way I never roared before,
And then I'd rrrwoof, and roar some more.
I would show the dinosaurus,
Who's king around the forres',
A king they better serve.
Why with my regal beezer
I could be another Caesar
If I only had the nerve.

5. "The Merry Old Land of Oz":
   There's a garden spot, I'm told,
   Where it's never too hot
   And it's never too cold;
   Where you're never too young
   And you're never too old,
   Where you're never too thin or tall.
   And you're never, never, never too,
   Too anything at all,
   Oh! you're not too mad
   And you're not too sane
   And you don't compare
   And you don't complain,
   All you do is just sit tight,
   'Cause it's all so, so, so downright, right . . .

6. "The Jitterbug":
   Listen all you chillun
   To that voo-doo moan,
   There's a modern villun

Worser than that old boogie woogie,
When that goofy critter
Spots your fancy clothes,
He injects a jitter,
Starts you dancing on a thousand toes,
There he goes.
Who's that hiding
In the tree top?
It's that rascal
The Jitterbug,
Should you catch him
Buzzing 'round you,
Keep away from
The Jitterbug.
Oh! the bees in the breeze
And the bats in the trees
Have a terrible, horrible buzz,
But the bees in the breeze
And the bats in the trees
Couldn't do what the Jitterbug does;
So be careful
Of that rascal,
Keep away from
The Jitterbug,
The Jitterbug,
The Jitterbug.
Oh! That Jitter,
Oh! The Bug,
Oh! The Jitterbug,
Bug-a-bug, bug-a-bug, bug-a-boo.
In a twitter,
In the throes,
Oh the critter's
Got me dancing on a thousand toes,
Thar she blows. . . .